CHARACTER GENERATION:
The Street Artist Method

Copyright © 2018 Jurg Bajiour

All rights reserved.

ISBN: 1987409817

ISBN-13: 978-1987409819

For Akasi & Anaji

CONTENTS

Preface	7
1. The Phantom Constituent	11
2. Masochism	23
3. Ritual Maintain	35
4. What's In A Name	53
5. Vandalism	69
6. Accessory To Utility	83
7. The Performance Artist	95
8. Busking	109
9. The Marks Of Passage	127
10. The Conservant	141

Preface:

A Note About This Edition:

Reading Character Generation as electronic media is commendable. The future is digital. The number of individuals who will employ the inexhaustive method seeded in this text on a digital visual platform probably exceeds the number of screenwriters, actors etc who will employ it as well. Reading a physical copy of Character Generation should come with the understanding that what one is in possession of is a limited edition original authenticable work of print art. For this edition, we've chosen one of the platforms democratizing the distribution of international standard book numbers to both digital and physical texts. Although a commercial entity, the equality that CreateSpace grants even the most disenfranchised artist or scribe is revolutionary. It is a part of the revolution in allocation of creative resources that includes CreatorSpace and Creative Commons. Both of which are non-profit organizations. The CreateSpace business model might prove unsustainable for a smaller company. Jim Yong Kim espoused the sentiment succinctly: "We need to look at every single way to bring in the private sector in order to maximize finance for development."

Chapter 1

The Phantom Constituent

[Constituent]

As an artist and a writer I am relatively open to communication. This may temper in time, but it has value that is neglected in the establishment creative community. Street Artist seek to maintain the integrity of our interactions through means that allow trust and general graciousness to build and endure without the detriment of inconvenience or inconsistency and without such casualty as rudeness or entitlement. #

When communicating with people without preamble, It is not unusual for me to get from them a gist of their reservation that no one is making it difficult for them to do this. I may feel the same way at a time, except that I am the representative of my work. When I write, it is for people to read. When I create art, it is for people to experience. The people who inadvertently give that vibe do not generally have a large body of work or are not artist or writers at all. Artist and writers have a partially self-serving responsibility to technically unsolicited inquiries from other artist and writers. Just as salesmen have an obligation to in-bound inquiries. #

When I as an artist or writer make an inquiry without preamble to another artist/writer I do so as a representative of my work and do not have a subconscious perception that it should be particularly difficult. In my experience it has not been such. Our artistic and journalistic/literary establishment has maintained this through the artistically involved and mediatistically involved minds of tiered agency. That is commendable in this business where exposure is a quantifiable asset. Progressive exposure can inspire episodic fanaticism in one's audience although that is not a sociological law and can as well be minimized. #

An art instructor may be inclined to ask their pupils 'Who is your artistic hero?' rather than 'Who is your favorite artist?'. Is the Street Artist an anti-hero? Will our Street Art establishment be anti-establishment? Instead of answering those questions let me direct the flow to a statement of deep significance. #

What we detail here as the Street Artist Method of Character Generation will assist you in developing a complex, modern and driven character without the predicate of a character arc or defining saga. As Interactive Media, Social Media and Collaborative Narrative in Art, Media and Entertainment perpetuate you will find this useful. You are often provided with Alias, Avatar or Blank Slate and as well with the tools to create the physical appearance of a character to your ideal. This method would like to engage, with you, tools and tenets to enhance the Realness of your character without consciously or subconsciously transposing merely your own trials, traits and aptitudes to them sans incorporating greater schemes, parallels and divergence. #

There is an expectation of realness that is inextricable from Street Artistry. The Street Artist is known to take a hands-on approach to agency. They are often observed bear-hugging their agent. But more importantly, they deign to remain artistically and mediatistically involved in agency. Here is an example of the artist treading into the journalist/writer's territory in the balance of our terminology. There is reciprocation, and journalist/writers may well preview Chapter 6: 'Accessory to

Utility' as they now go as far as to parallel the Street Artist complete with ascending casual handle and it is described there within. I will encourage you not to 'preview'. I'm attempting to throw you off of spoilers thus mentioning that the scribe, photog and videographer are party to this entire text. There will be no scribe-journo vs photo-journo kind of elaboration so just know that we party the Journo well. The streets ordain. #

Artist of the new millennium give credence to every communicative aspect of any new ascendant application. You only have to look at the once 'insider notion' of 'push notification' to know that developers give particular credence to the communicative aspects of competitive applications. The push notification is a specific communicative mechanism. Without limiting ourselves to that, let us zero in on some examples of communicative mechanism relevant to artist today. We will form a well-rounded conception but doubtlessly eschew unique and emerging functions of various standard and new applications. #

I will identify the applications by presently deserved superlatives. A discussion-changing application encourages communication through messages directed, though not precisely direct, to an individual or entity. The message can be searched and viewed by most anyone. A public-face-changing application allows for messages even on public pages which do not rely on the usual (to that app) two-party confirmation. The business changing application is comparatively sparse in its uber-direct intimations and acknowledgments thus they stand out as significant communications. #

It gets less cut and dry. The notification, when used ingeniously, is one of the most useful facets of a new application. Why not specify the technological nature of the forums of which we speak? Most reasonably because these can be translated to a group of people in the same room delegating the modality with which they pass paper notes between one another. Most realistically because mode is ever changing and medium is ever evolving. #

A source changing app specific to the music industry innovates brief observations pinned to the precise moment in the duration of a musical work that the notifying party found or finds most appropriate. A rep changing app; that is, it changes the dynamics of user to user self-representation; goes so far as to include an 'ask' communication allowing visitor questions which are both useful and non-cumbersome to engage. Blogs, popular social video media and many sites allow for comments posted anonymously or specifically. 'Comments' in their basic form are the least relevant to the artist communicative mechanism. #

Two digressive yet canny observations. 1) A talented and popular columnist for a major weekly news magazine once lamented that "Commenters are killing web 2.0" 2) A talented and popular recording artist once asked the developer of the top photo-sharing app if they might, putting their heads together, "Clean Up" the interface. #

Notice the words 'pinned' and 'ask' being tantamount to our well rounded conception. They are key and even *titular* in unmentioned applications that already compete boldly in the field and they indeed are entirely different/particular from the others. #

Without going further as such, the last couple of these are well established so we are naturally through with superlatives. A communication changing device, indeed application, allows for... excuse me, email allows for concrete messages between two parties. #

What makes a party fit the semantic usage of the word? What makes it more than just a gathering together? Is it a situation where the individuals in attendance are guaranteed to focus their interactions on things that will tickle and titillate them? Is the consumption of alcohol mandated to forge a modality of interaction not found elsewhere in daily life? Are the modes of affection and attenuation generally premeditated by party hosts reserved for and inclined to catalyze interrelations that otherwise would not manifest? #

Apologies. I'm homonym friendly. These things happen. #

What makes a party fit the semantic usage of the word? The other party. Your party of 'more than one' yes. Your party of as many as humanly possible. Yes that one. Are you rife with intention wrent from your values and poli-philosophical in nature? Are you a veritable wall of sound indivisible from your core intentions and indomitable by design? Do you maintain vocally, fight valiantly, and leave quietly? Why quietly? Are you aware that the responsibilities of a civil servant are indeed to serve? And besides you totally introduced "The Next President of the Union" and in hindsight that title was not absolutely one-hundred-percent correct. #

It's worth noting that presidents in North America and elsewhere steadfastly refrain from criticizing the policies of their successor. The civil servant can be said to parallel the Street Artist, whose approach to art is from a place of Social Purpose and Social Justice in greater abundance than any previous school of artistic inclination. It is expressly due to such purpose that Street Art appreciators are not just inclined to artistic reserve in the presence of their most appreciated provident artist, they are inclined to mediatic revere. With a bit of prodding from the veritable idol, they'll often erupt into (gender-less) fraternity. #

The Street is invariably a socially marginalized arena and Street Artist inevitably have more facets of lifestyle in common and less inequality between them than other successful artist in the presence of their preoccupational counterpart. They tend to get on quite well. The complementary nature of the artistic ambitions of the Street Art consumer (let's use engagor) is another reason for the absence of fanaticism in their interaction. #

Constituent, in the arena of politics, refers to the voting body that elected a particular official. There is an old jest likening the constituent's influence to the tough love of a parent i.e. they brought you into this world and can take you out of it. When we allegorically replace electoral process with commerce, the "dire" voter need for recourse to action is unrequited. Fortunately art is more rooted in honesty than any other comparatively self-starting profession. I invite you to debate that point but will meet your philosopher, clergy, and historian with a titter, a laugh, and a hyperventilation. #

Honesty is not a fail-proof model for engagement and thus the Artist must find ways to convey their perspective with aesthetic appeal. A politician's peril in alienating his constituent is absolute. If an artist took an oath of occupation it might say s/he promises to challenge, unnerve and surprise his/her supportive body in addition to champion and illuminate them. We know those 3 former notions would force a recall election if they reared their head in the political arena, but artist are not immune to the prospect of alienating their supportive body. #

A popular graphic artist recently made intolerant statements during a time-frame where his tomes were being adapted into narrative films. The backlash in popular social media and popular media was immediate and extreme. Furthermore, from what I could discern, the third installment of the film adaptations of his work had a distinctly less sensational box office draw. #

Social Purpose and Social Justice are age-old tenets of Street Art. Art has rarely ever been less reliant on popular media than during this advent of Street Art. Whereas Revolutionary Artist throughout history have often used media outrage to their advantage, Street Art has occupied a place where any media outrage is more or less irrelevant. The Street Artist is, to an overwhelming degree, nonplussed by hysteria. The reasons for this are vast. One obvious point of study is that a defining medium/style of the various forms is, to this day, considered criminal. A faulty generalization. We will elaborate in Chapter 5. #

A party will generally share common interests. How it goes about increasing its mass is much less guilded. The examples of Whigs vs Tories and of Democratic Republicans being semantically lopped in half by Democrats are much less interesting than the Working Families Party, the LGBTQXYZ Party, the Rent Is Too Damn High Party and the like. If you'll recall your civics lessons, a party platform is made up of planks. The planks are made up of the numerous political-suicides that walked bound and blindfolded off the edge of it. #

When an Artist makes a political statement, it is much less interested in divergent feedback than a politician. Divergent responses to a political statement are natural. Artist, however, seek that far less than the humble civil servant. Reaching consensus is actually the politicians entire challenge. They challenge you to reach consensus. They will even lead one position to assure that there is due process. #

The artist goes even further wherein the interrelation of wo/man and constituent gains play. The Artist frequently and the Street Artist prevalently seek to challenge your preconceived notions. These notions are generally more elaborate than would elicit a polarized or divergent response from a randomly sampled group of people. In rare cases, however, art can elicit a polarized and divergent reaction as simple as "should this be displayed?" #

I am only partially making light of a serious concern by saying: Traditionally individuals who have the divergent response in our example, react by taking the art home with them to consider it. Artist have become cautious of that inanity since their own time is put into the art and really "who does such a fanatic think he is?" If he forthrightly believes himself a civil servant or happens to be an official of the governing body, repercussions may ensue. It's better just to make a legal transaction with all who remove a work of art from the display area. #

It is also of tradition not to offend the senses of your audience and lead them to pilfer your art or even summon an official of the governing body to seize it. This method allows the artist the opportunity to elicit more responses to the same or additional art that is presented in an attributable way. #

Considering the fact that your audience has the potential to include people who may attest to having an enforceable position on how or whether your art should be displayed, and particularly in public areas, it should stand to reason that imagining a phantom constituent can help further an artistic pursuit. If not pursuit as an artist, pursuit as a commercial entity. Drawing revenue from one's art is a method for sustaining the time, the need for other occupations considered, to create art. #

Signing a work of art is both common and uncommon depending on the mediums you are comparing. It is a traditional way of attributing the art to an identifiable artist or collective. Representation or reintroduction of an element within given works of art is also a traditional method of attribution. Informal or formal attribution is a requisite for the commercial utilization of art. #

Final paragraph:

One of the most useful techniques for getting a speculative script past the various stages of acceptance to the point of green-lighting and production of the feature film, is the unilateral character empathy tip. There are limits to its viability, usually where the inability to empathize with a character is a part of the underlying appeal of the story arc. Although this has seen recent success, it is considered somewhat shticky. Even where super-villains are concerned, without a shred of humanity, a character is academically considered underdeveloped. In screenwriting, playwriting, and improvisational acting; where there are clear and present hurdles to the art being accepted and reaching its finished form, empathy is the creator's tool. The clear and present difficulty for an improvised character is in the immediate reaction of observers. Most comic performers and improv artist know that without a healthy dose of empathy from the audience, humor is almost impossible. In writing for the stage and screen, we instruct authors to edit their work with each significant character in mind. If it is someone you personally have little empathy with, you need to consider those who do empathize with him or her. A Fireman who turns to Arson for example, is very unlikely to go the distance to production if the work is read by a former Fireman and the Fireman character turns him or her off completely. The decisions, circumstances, and actions of a character have to tow the line of believability precisely where his or her like observers would look for it. This applies, in the same way, to their mannerisms, vocalisms and overall temperament. This applies, in the same way, to their grooming, dressing, and overall appearance.

Chapter 2

Masochism

[Masochism]

An individual's deliberate impression on their mind and body are two facets of the instinctual inclination toward self identification. The human being learns very early in its interaction with its ex-utero environment that pain is the body's chief indicator of external stimuli with the capacity to change the organism's physical self. This is the case for the mind, but in terms of mental processes. They can be altered, even against will, by pain 'part and parcel' due some stimuli mental or physical. #

The bounds of pain are very strict. The extreme register encompasses torture and stimuli that the body avoids transmitting as pain by going into shock. The low end of the scale goes as far as mild discomfort. The human being, like most mammals, exist in a state of relative painlessness. Being warm blooded, maintaining that idyllic environment is phenotypical. Observable enduring impressions on the body can be literally useful in the continued performance or creation of works of art. They can just as well be useful in the continued performance of an occupation or a kind of work. Masochistic pain can indeed inform an individual to engage it again most simply if it conditions the body to be resistant to that pain. #

The bounds of mental pain are less strictly partitioned but they are generally indicated by intensity of stress. Torture is also the extreme register. The low end of the scale encompasses mental discomforts not often perceived as pain. It is important that these stimuli be included regarding pain because incisive and coercive contradictions of Will can alter an organism's mental processes. Sublimation and the recently achieved mind to mind remote manipulation of physical movements etc fall into a category outside the immediate and important notion of pain. #

The International Human Rights Commission designates certain extreme forms of treatment as Torture and they are Universally Outlawed. In the study of Street Artistry we should consider Masochism not as the complementary to Sadism, but as the oppositional to Hedonism. The pursuit of pleasure–or–pleasure seeking is not unilaterally or generally disdained by Street Artist. However, the translation of the facets of personal pain is a long-held tenet of revolutionary art. #

The deliberate impression on the mind or body of an individual's self does not preclude stimulus that do not leave a physical mark or observable enduring mental/physical effect. It is a natural inclination that attends to the individual's separation from its environment. Here's an example. When completely isolated for abnormally elongated periods of time, there are diminishments in the common traits of self-perception. In such absence of others, a human being is inclined to relegate speech to a point where it is difficult to utilize it when reintroduced to others. The difficulty can be as great as or even greater than attempting to communicate with people who don't speak the individual's known languages. #

In abnormally elongated isolation, a person's interaction with its environment undergo various changes that resemble the dynamics of earlier stages of the organism's Social Evolution. These changes qualify as observable enduring mental effects. Some of these changes (veritable "disconnects") can be more casually understood by comparison to various states of narration. In '3rd person' narration, an individual speaks of himself "Yours truly, Jean-Michel doesn't know where he's hanging out tonight". In '1st person' an individual speaks of another "Jean doesn't know where is gettin down tonight". In '2nd person' an individual speaks of you "You don't know where you're kicking it tonight, Jean". #

Listen, Jean, why don't you just read my book tonight? The likelihood of Jean responding "Jean-Michel isn't reading any book tonight!" is a rare response during elongated isolation, though it is a frequent reemergence immediately after reintegration in contrast to our general disuse and even humor about '3rd person' self-reference. #

The '1st person' is the first facet to be relegated and even altogether discarded in the absence of other individuals. If you are isolated, even when holding internal conversations with your self-talk there is little reason to talk about what your friend Jean is doing or not doing. #

The '2nd person' is the longest enduring but also delible form of interpersonal reference in elongated isolation. Say to yourself "you're not reading any book tonight". That style of self-talk becomes the standard parameter of "conversational dialogue" in the isolated person's existence. #

The previous observations help to explain the reemergence of '3rd person' self-reference during an individual's reintegration into society. But bear in mind, Name is often an eventual casualty of elongated isolation. The necessity to distinguish between people is removed and thus Name gives way to pronoun and pronoun even gives way to pronoun-less internal speech. "Not reading any book tonight." #

Self-Isolation is a frequently engaged ritual of artist. We will discuss ritual further in the next chapter (3). Our fascinating example should also inform our understanding of the word 'deliberate' in this chapter and in this text. I use it here in illustrating the potentials of conditioning to the mind. It does that well. Masochism and forms of stress-based conditioning and pain-based conditioning leave much of the cognitive process to the subconscious. Yet, as per our example, you can observe that the subconscious is potentially reacting very elaborately to the conditioning stimulus. Our example is also utilized to illustrate that "deliberate" impressions are not necessarily 'intentional' impressions. They are more so 'observable' impressions. One may not mean to isolate themselves yet benefit from it. One may not mean to be internally stressed by being alone yet change or grow from it. #

The instinctual inclination toward self identification tends against the subject-diminishing effects of isolation. That is to say that people create art with the intention of sharing it. People often seek to have their art attributed to them. People often intend that their art be purchased or accepted and admired in absence of the artist. Isn't it interesting that we often intend that our artwork, admired in our absence, elicit an admiration that does not consciously reference the artist when re-experiencing. Reference to the artist, in many mediums and forms that do not require the artist's physical self, physical image, or distinct vocal representation is primarily to marry the notions of art and commerce. It can also be to marry the notions of art and fanatical commerce-less obsession with the artist. Or preferably the milder versions of attention on that spectrum. #

It is important to know that in our present social systems, appreciation of art causes appreciation in value of that art even if not directly benefiting the artist. Just as ignorance of art causes ignorance in value of that art even if not directly denigrating the artist. #

An individual's deliberate impression on its mind or body is a way in which the intention toward individuality and individual identity is preserved. The effects of deliberate impressions are observable by the individual and, potentially, others. Physical and mental deliberate impressions occur through a range of action, but their permanence is often correlative to the pain or stress caused during the stimulus. Pain and stress being, generally, facets of that impression. Pain does not preclude stress nor vice versa. #

An individual's deliberate impression on its mind or body will be a notion we dwell on periodically in this text. It does not pain me to point out, the instinctual inclination toward self identification is often art in elabor. Or more beautifully; it is often, in elabor, art. Simple definitions of art are hard to come by. I wouldn't suggest getting too attached to that one considering we haven't yet touched on deliberate impressions on one's environment. (More on that, and on attribution in Chapter 5: 'Vandalism'.) As definitions go it seems to preclude impressions intended to identify other places, people, etc. #

Greater Humanity wants you to live in relative painlessness. Not 'live it up' or live wastefully, but to 'not be dying'. Pain, often of a mentally or physically stressful nature, precedes the event of dying in a great proportion of instances outside of 'natural causes' as we've termed it. One can intuitively assume that pain's function is to guide the individual away from scenarios that may lead to its death. Circumstances of both physical and mental "pain" should fall under such scenarios. As we stated, mental 'pain' is harder to define than physical 'pain'. The general concept of Masochism elaborates on the blurring of the bounds between physical pain and physical pleasure. Here, we append the often neglected, obviously blurred, bounds between mental pain and mental pleasure as well. #

Here is an important question. Wherefore pain (by responsive avoidance) is intended to help promote the longevity of an organism. And wherefore if it is difficult to distinguish between pain and pleasure, 'How does one determine if a certain sensational experience is to be worked against or itself promoted?' After all, 'Work' can well be painful. #

I can move to a certain city in a certain country north of my present city and present country and get the equivalent of 300 USD a month. For nothing. For existing. For getting there and acquiring a residence. When Greater Humanity can accomplish such a thing as that, it hopes to make one see work as an incentive. Work promotes the individual from resident to responsible civilian or even citizen if they go through certain familiarizing processes. Citizens and even responsible civilians have a vested interest in their community's political process. They often vote. #

We are all somewhere on "earth" at present to speak of humanity in an informal way. We can potentially plant our food throughout our surroundings and need nearly nothing from government and mass commerce. Greater Humanity knows this. The notion that if you can not work you should be dying is a capitalistic ill. #

The greater humanity and the greater sustainability are inextricable concepts. It is because of the greater sustainability that the greater humanity is able to maintain a selfless perspective. The greater humanity risks becoming less relevant and potentially irrelevant if it loses the selfless core of its perspective. #

Having used cognitive juxtapositions that veritably describe my geographical reality, earlier in this chapter, let me indicate a change in time here. I am continuing with this chapter for the first time since being specific about place earlier. Anything can have changed during that time. As well, any chapter in this text may have been appended to since then. Considering the evolving nature of occupation, my professional relationship with Street Art may have changed. But whatever the case, the relevant points of this chapter will remain unchanged. Masochism involves deliberate impressions on the mind or body with intent to condition. It is important to note that "Work" often accomplishes the same. #

The Right to Work, which is limited, should not be confused with the notion that if you can not work you should be dying. The former is a catch-phrase used by some industrialized social systems to encourage undocumented emigrants that they will not be immediately prosecuted for taking menial jobs often for below the established minimum wages. The latter is an ill that capitalism can further export, given the influence over culture. #

Regarding the so called 'right to work' there is irony in the preference given to immigrants over minority citizens for the menial occupations mentioned earlier. This is the case in many industrialized nations. This is in part because of the exploitative wages the employers would like to pay and tax-free when possible, and due to institutionalized racism. Learning how to avoid taxes and responsibility, forging affiliations to capitalize on that avoidance, moving on from menial labor, the exponential value of industrial wages when sent to an immigrant's family abroad, and the unregulated nature of capitalizing on that value all contribute to the undocumented immigrants ability to prosper far beyond the minority citizen. #

Many, many people can directly benefit from the revenue of a business that only requires one documented citizen to license. The beneficiaries do not have to keep their distance by virtue. They also can forgo conforming to the values and morés of the new society often by sheer avoidance. One of the primary effects of the human tendency to evolve together in social systems, is the mitigation of an individual's propensity toward heterogeneity. Resistance to deviance. I will mention this again in Chapter 9: 'The Marks of Passage'. #

There is an old saying that 'doing the same thing and expecting a different result' is masochism. This is perhaps true, but it is not the form of masochism that we are studying in this text. The masochism of responsive self-conditioning is not the masochism of psychopathy. Industrialized nations take note. #

Before ever government programs like Social Security were introduced to enable helping to provide for people once they became too elderly to compete in the global workforce, social systems exhibited that were intended to do similar things. Arranged Marriages are an example of a social construct that is chosen to benefit those wedding and both wedding parties. Yet our patriarchal power dynamics can leave the bride's benefit far below all else. It can even be her detriment. #

It is well known that the time we occupy with our physical work is an accelerated permutation of our individual selves designed to provide for the rest and recreation of individuals. As it is that any vigorous physical action repeated, exercise included, causes noticeable strain to the body and can even initiate chronic pain, there are common adjective relationships between an individual and work that inevitably help to identify more elaborate tendencies in the individual. #

Aloofness is more useful than laziness in mitigating the allocation of tasks to the individual while maintaining a certain bounty of occupational validity. The neurotic are generally vastly mitigating physical pain while embellishing their threshold for mental discomfort. Workaholism generally uses one of the two facets of masochism in order to fulfill the accelerated permutation of self that is Individual Occupation. #

In the instance that one's occupation is that of an artist, Workaholism can still utilize one of the two facets of masochism. The two being deliberate impressions on the mind or on the body. We'll elaborate that with a useful example or two in Chapter 7: 'The Performance Artist'. #

Final paragraph:

Consider the fact that learning is a more complex cognitive behavioral process than most forms of conditioning, those relying on masochism included. Artist Athletes, for example a Choreographer or Martial Artist, are not the only kind of artist that can benefit from conditioning. Street Art can be used to immediately call to mind a character whose artistic propensity toward masochism resembles our stereotypical notions of masochism as responsive conditioning. That is to say, the stereotypical cognitive behavioral response that instructs us "do not do this during your art or performance because it hurts". If your artist is an Extreme Athlete they will typically engage that simple responsive conditioning during the process of learning their difficult routines, moves and maneuvers. Consider your character's desire to learn and what motivates it to desire to learn a certain skill or understanding. Consider the fact that human beings make an effort to allow their motivations to maintain a greater favor than their inclinations. If your character has a profession, occupation, or otherwise a job distinct from a non-occupational study; consider your character's desire to work and what motivates it. Consider how your character demonstrates the effort to allow its motivations to maintain greater favor than their inclinations.

Chapter 3

Ritual Maintain

[Ritual]

The instinctual inclination toward self identification can be examined via 5 basic facets: An individual's deliberate impression on their mind, body, environment, other individuals and greater humanity. We use 'greater humanity' here to remain inclusive of fauna and civilizations foreign to any immediate civilization of reference. Humanity is, at its core, vastly inclusive. Sustainability has evolved to represent a similar responsibility to the flora and the environment with its many cycles and sensitivities. #

Artist, and Street Artist in particular, are acutely aware of the responsibility of individuals to the Greater Humanity and the Greater Sustainability. #

The conservationist and the humanitarian are still marginal as of the writing of this text. Despite the emphasis on service by academic, religious and social organizations; despite high-society's cult of philanthropy; despite the upper-middle class social dependence on the personal-responsibility or social-responsibility; despite the deeply ingrained appeal of samaritans and heroes; Humanity and Sustainability are both underdogs. #

An important part of man or woman's deliberate impression on its own mind is the way it perceives itself in relation to its society. Given the various homogeneities of a society that are easily recognizable to members of that society, the man or woman in question generally seeks to occupy a place where they are subconsciously confident they can be recognized by fellow member of their society for their (mutually) appreciable traits. This tendency toward 'typifying' is a frequent component of the homogeneity we witness in our societies. #

In the artist, the tendency toward 'typifying' one's 'deliberate impression on their own mind' serves a complex purpose. It is not only with the intention of fitting in, but as well to circumvent an initial phase of mediatic alienation from the artist and art by an experiencing audience. In admitting traits with which they identify, the artist ushers like personalities closer, and insulates less familiar personalities against potential surprises in the art. This is highly significant considering the universal tenet of 'honesty' in professional artistry. #

Realness is a tenet of Street Art. It refers to any facet of expression or commonality of or pertaining to that which is inborn socially as opposed to actively acquired. It is, in effect, honesty of representation. It is less contingent on the individual and gives a more distinct and immediate reference to an individual's artistic community. #

There is prevalent misuse of and misunderstanding of the concept of realness. The prominent origination of its usage is in the lexicon of hip hop as a multifaceted art form. Today, a digital media company has made an issue of the most abundantly search optimized photo sharing application. Search optimization being the user intention and abundance of hash-tagging being the user method. The article lightly states that #funeral is the realest hash-tag on the application. #

The understanding is that people are very serious at funerals and this falls in line with the "realness" that is implored specifically by 1990s gangster rap and by the 2000s new-money rap. In a matter of fact the phrase "keep it real" is even older in hip hop and was used even in 80s compositions and spoken language. #

Realness is one of those necessary and utile concepts that in its infancy invites the 'toying with' of it conjugations and meanings. But all that is just can't just be self-justified. Obviously that's obvious. #

However, the instruction "keep it real" and its various permutations were intended to foster something other than stoicism. Fakeness is not just pretense. It is habitual behavior that paves the way for exploitation. Therefore the unyielding frequency of realness in Street Art is part of the community ritual that promotes the community's values. Honesty of representation is policed by reducing the individual ability to self-justify in favor of group dynamic. #

The media company indicates #funeral as one of many "realest hashtags" as we are fond of superlative hyperbole in our present digital media. The confusion with realness is not as cartoon as the examples one pulls for study. The danger of exploitative renditions brings to the cautious numerous defensive observations. The intention of discerning "real life" from the commercialized and/or attention craving glut is commendable, yet superficial reasoning exacerbates exploitation. I've encountered the confusion and misguiding usage in other places. #

The word maintain in ritual maintain refers not only to the continuation of a ritual, but as well to the relatively involved concept of maintain as it is common in street etiquette primarily in the process of salutation. Trending expansively via the influence of hip hop monologue and dialogue, it is a concept within the universal working class wherein the inclination toward progress is a shared sentiment. There is the innate understanding that progress does not necessarily manifest in obvious ways, and that the spoils of working class progress in the aggressive capitalist system often go toward keeping things as they are whereas things would otherwise fall into despair and dilapidation. #

Taken in that essence Maintain is the root word of our title and ritual is its modifier. Not only would one say that they are 'maintainin' in response to an interrogative greeting such as "how are you doing", one might also inform that they are 'maintainin with their peoples' when contacted remotely at a gathering or shared location. That usage further elaborates the communal nature and human face of 'maintain' unlike, say, ritual maintenance. It quite literally means holding together and supporting one another. #

We, however, opt for syntactic ambiguity in our titular head. Ritual is a well-known interpersonal tendency that is often referenced when attempting to lend depth to a description of someone or shed light on the character of a subject. It is important in our title both as keyword and as modifier. The modifier ritual denotes consistency or even continuity of action. #

When I began this text, The Greater Humanity and The Greater Sustainability were not conscious observations in my internal self-talk. They leapt out (probably during my study of Conservancy) and found their first mention here in Ritual Maintain and second via elaboration of a point made in Masochism. I wrote more than 50% of this volume before noticing that Humanity and Sustainability were intrinsic parts of Ritual Maintain and subsequently arriving at this very paragraph where I would begin to elaborate. Humanity and Sustainability. Not the Greater Humanity and the Greater Sustainability. Just the basic forms. #

We maintain with humanity and sustainability. It is not lost on me that the semantics are precise in their parallel with the way we use the term today. I do not maintain my peoples. I do not maintain via my peoples. I maintain with my peoples. In the same way, it is much more defining and encompassing to maintain with humanity and sustainability, than it is to maintain them or to maintain via them. #

The city in which I presently reside is in a crisis of humanity and sustainability. The reasons for this are many. Unfortunately analyzing them overemphasizes victim-hood when the blame of my fellow city-folk should not be underscored. #

The consequences of a lack of humanity toward even one person can be dire for the entire humanity. The consequences of an insustainability agenda toward one individual can be dire for the entire sustainability. #

The notion that inhumanity and the oppression of someone's

livelihood will shift the burden of courtesy and fairness to others, is a pathetic fallacy. As in literature, those who are "gross with conviction" and are the slaves of "fate" are prone to pathetic fallacy. The poet who thinks his love can simply be described as the sun & rain or a flowers bloom is intoxicated in a benevolence without him. #

Courtesy and fairness are the responsibility of all people. When people remove courtesy and fairness from interaction, they are well aware of the exponent value of their action. An exponent devalue to be precise. By defying the expectation of simple universal respect, they hope to preoccupy their target's moral rumination for much longer than the moment it took them to act out. Often, as their observation of the target's disconcertion and moral rumination notes satisfying vastness, they seek to utilize the same weapon at a different moment in the hopes of 'provoking' their target. #

Incisive and coercive intonations, interjections, and commentary are considered rude and tempered with preamble and apology for good reason. The intent to elicit rumination and preoccupation is inherent. We are autonomous beings. We do not requite the moment to moment direction of others. The city of reference has taken those incisions and coercions to a new level and have shown that such distractions are in fact dangerous. They reduce the mind's capacity to tend to the details of their own survival and they do so as a Contradiction of Will. #

The intent to influence perceptions others have of an individual is also inherent. Rudeness subversively and universally devalues an individual and the society in which they live. It calls into question our recourse to policing. #

The conspiratorial oppression of the livelihood of one man can throw into disbalance the sustainability of an entire social system. As it is that our lives as individuals with certain individual identities have a beginning and an end, there is no amount of time that merit can be oppressed without a lasting detriment to the individual and the place that individual occupies in the Greater Humanity. #

The same applies to the oppression, intentional or misguided, of the livelihood of women. In our yet patriarchal business world, it is quite conspiratorial. I bring this up because this is a prime area to discuss the maligning of merit through a less conspiratorial process. Either scenario can befall either gender, but let us examine. #

The tendency of new fathers of young women to set a different patriarchal agenda for the lives of their daughters than they would their sons is prevalent. The reasons for this are many. The awareness of and wariness toward the disparity in women's incomes versus men's is one reason. In some social systems, very occupations for women are scarce. But an agenda to coddle and provide for one's daughter for her entire life, instead of goading her to demand the equivocal desert of her merit, is shortsighted in more ways than one. #

The continual prevalence of fairy tale allegories in the rearing of children is harmful. Obviously, the subjection and submission to feudal princes and princesses and their presumed divine lineage and divine right is harmful to everyday people. But these tales have an enduring effect on motivation and expectation that leads to a skewed perspective on merit based prosperity. #

Skewed perspectives on merit are an area that warrants further study. I have written a bit more on several different chapters of this volume before this paragraph was written. At the same time, I have relocated to a different city and may well remain there as the remaining 25% of this tome is rendered from my mind. #

As empathy would have it, the fortification of negative habits is detectable and moving from place to place doesn't immediately and definitively extricate from your life the negative emotive you have come into contact with. #

Skewed perspectives on merit manifest variously in the lives of much of society. However, such mentalities are not following the course of operative social systems. #

Subconscious conditioning that is permitted to pervade the lives of adults despite its origins in intensively marketed trappings of their youth does not follow the course of operative social systems. A social construct can not be a viable part of a social system if when it comes against catalyst for change it resists instead of adapting. #

An Ironic manifestation of a skewed perspective on merit that demonstrated itself to a frustrating degree in the city I formerly wrote from, is the equating of love and sex that, in effect, imbued aesthetic appreciation with not just the residual emotive due aesthetic attraction, but as well the residual emotive due enduring complementary appreciation. #

The nuance of Enduring Complementary Appreciation is difficult to utilize in relation to a stranger. There are exceptions for those occasions where the stranger will prove to be your significant other or life partner. If it was a function of a desperation to fulfill their recreational social purpose of having a partner for me amongst them, that would be one thing. It was a different kind of misuse of amygdala by the empathic. Extremely frustrating and, by its prevalence, an indicator of a skewed if not irreparably warped perspective on merit. #

Even under the guise of such deceptive jests, the prevalence of a warped conception of the difference between love and sex is widespread in 'popular' culture. It has enduring effects that may not manifest as the root of complex problems that arise in human relationships, partly because the root of those problems is generally isolated as a distinct consideration that can not be so simply defined. #

It is very simple to separate the emotive for aesthetic appreciation, aesthetic attraction, and enduring complementary appreciation. To do so for yourself, and refuse to do so for another individual as you witness an encounter in that individual's life, is criminal-maniacal social behavior. Such tendencies are indicative of a more severe type of sociopathy than general cheating, lying and backstabbing. #

Power, in general is a faulty social construct that systems like Democracy were designated to help mitigate. In fact, an ideal political system would eliminate the overbearing dependence on power and thus lessen resulting obsessions with the concept. Wherein superstition is the primary category for the credence given to chance encounters and their contingent responsive conditioning, there is an awareness in the superstitious of 'Power' as a social construct that is furthermore enticingly immediate and potentially satisfying to devotion. It is entirely unsustainable however. #

Gambling, much like dabbling in fatalism or sorcering one's superstition, is mathematically unsustainable. It is intended to have an identifiable payout. I could have as well used the phrase 'toying with fate'. None of the above are incorrect statements, none the less. #

The laws of mathematics reveal affirmations of most such gambles to be the natural fortunes of chance. However, the desire to have an overreaching effect on another person's life, particularly in a negative way, and emotional addiction to that "power" is an evolved form of sociopathy that is criminal-maniacal in nature. #

Addiction to 'Power' has repeatedly proven itself to be inhumane geopolitically. But even on the small scale of social interaction it is often criminal-maniacal. Social media's maligning of the publicist in favor of more continuous interaction with celebrated personalities has proven itself a haven for inhumanity. Simple communication can access the nodes of power and control through hyperbole/euphemism, expletive, insult and like notions. A hyperbolic or euphemistic statement designed to caricature or ridicule a person is not immediately an insult, but it is immediately abusive. I am highly interested that a Big Data cruncher among you my peers and pupils would: divine for me how many comments, that can be deemed negative and were directed at celebrated personalities, included not one but *all* three of those things. Hyperbole or Euphemism being one. #

Humanity and Sustainability can not be excluded from the viable constructs of a working social system. #

We will further discuss the potentials of celebrated personalities directing their charity toward 'experiential' awareness raising and fundraising, in Chapter 7: 'The Performance Artist'. But let me clearly indicate that by the time of this final edit, a full-on Revolution is underway in the euro-american entertainment industry and business world, and it is turning the patriarchal establishment on its head. High profile terminations and resignations are far, far into the double digits. These are men who were abusing their positions for sexual favor, accedence, and even violence. These are companies that were allowed to pay women far less than men for equal work. This is what we have long meant by colloquial terms like "break the glass ceiling" and "smash the patriarchy". Today we are doing it. #

We maintain not just with our fam (as we have somewhat extended the definition of family in our slang), we maintain with our peers and coworkers. Internet democratisation of media is a cornerstone of the above stated revolution. In this interconnected age, we maintain with our heroes. #

But let me delve one layer deeper into an issue that arises within the fam. The continual prevalence of fairy tale allegories in the rearing of children happens to be a thing that has a contingent effect on the tendency of new fathers of young women to set a different patriarchal agenda for the lives of their daughters than they would their sons. The stratification of reason is not as obvious as the semantics of that statement may lead you to attempt deduction. #

The father of a young child rarely perceives themselves as someone who "believes in" fairy tales. The difficulty and prosaicness of child rearing and of maintaining with one's newly biological-parenthood-based relationship generally brings sufficient doses of reality to all involved. #

But it is imperative to note that the agenda to coddle and provide for one's daughter for her entire life, still comes from the 'belief' in fairy tales none the less. There are many stories of adults who were adopted as children falling in love with and even marrying their biological parent later in their life. The phenomenon of an individual altering the emotive due enduring complementary appreciation between parent and child and conceiving it as actually the emotive due enduring complementary appreciation between life partners is not limited to those who are first acquainted as adults. It can happen within a parents conception of their relation with their young child as they observe his/her growth. #

The reasons for the misallocation of emotive, and consequently misallocation of thought given to helping plan for the child's future, are rooted in a fatalist belief in the sentience of 'true love'. Whereas the fairy tale romance between the individual and the child's other parent has revealed its prosaicness, a new opportunity for 'fairy tale love' is arising. The liberal example of divorced men wedding women they knew as young girls when they themselves were by contrast full grown adults, is a significant extreme to examine. #

Not at the point we are discussing, but certainly by the time the child is finishing school, thoughts of their living forever with the parent will be history in most, but not all, societies. Wherein parents are already considered senior citizens by the time a child is beyond schooling, an enduring complementary relationship of co-habitation and generally co-occupation is known to require few other habitation/occupation scenarios outside of the rite of passage. #

Most importantly, one who feels a greater Enduring Complementary Appreciation for a child than for their partner (perhaps the other parent of that child), should do well to feel a distinct responsibility for the relative grandchild. You are, after all, taking that responsibility in the event of making choices that mute the child's social advancement yet provide for them throughout their life. It becomes hard to calculate let alone to fulfill the amount of provident care necessary for several generations one supposedly appreciates more than they would allow to suffer occupations, or worse, convenient relationships. But to do anything less when initiating a dependent social construct with your child would be inhumane to that child's emotional well being and as well inhumane to the human being that would be your grandchild. The difficulty calculating the necessary providence leads me to believe it should be insustainable as well. #

Marriage is not an occupation. You might endeavor to see any occupation that requires more responsibility than your marriage as an extreme. Raising your children is not an occupation and any occupation that requires less responsibility than raising your children is quite necessarily encouraging you to help with childrearing and homemaking and maybe even allow your spouse to return to work. That's a lot of occupations. You know what to do. #

Heading volunteer organizations for minimal or no pay has been the social niche of the wives of wealthy (and/or publicly prominent) members of civil society. However, in some societies "Work" is very limited (read: restricted) for women often taking place primarily in the home or family trade. Of course in Agricultural societies women are as often the backbone of the family trade as men. Being a homemaker is often idealized as the easiest possible responsibility. It is most frequently none such thing. Women often take that responsibility *while* working in a family trade. The notion that the wife of a wealthy man should feel so unfulfilled by the innecessity of her working as to work for free for a volunteer organization, is alien to much of the world. #

Although the family unit is by no means the only viable primary social system for an individual to transverse his or her earliest maturing years in, it is a dominant one in human civilizations. We maintain with our families first and foremost. Dispensing with a patriarchal family structure is much easier to accomplish scientifically and sociologically than dispensing with the matriarchal family structure. The matriarchal structure coexists with the patriarchal and, more often than otherwise, exists in its absence. #

Ritual, in human conception, is a feminine construct where great importance is placed on process to which results are not immediate or overt. Even when applied to a hyper-masculine activity such as hunting, it incorporates feminine energy to that which would inspire assumptions to the contrary. Ritual is present and overt in every part of reproduction from courtship to childrearing. #

There is 'maintainin' in the rituals of reproduction. Even the most callous thug maintained with his mother or surrogate for 9 undisputed months. They were like for-real cuzins. After birth and nurturing, we as families hope to incorporate some measure of free will into the lives of young men and women. We hope that maintainin with them for prior lengths can be of eventual benefit to us, but there is no guarantee. #

Final Paragraph:

Consider that the growing of plants is the most widespread occupation on earth. I am here separating this from farming. The Utilitarian perspective on human consumption believes that the raising of livestock can be ethical and the only obstacle to that is the adoption of humane enclosure and painless euthanasia. There is a school of thought that insists that there is No way to be humane and ethical when you are ending the life of an animal that does not want to die. This argument, which we haven't yet risen to the level of practically, is rendered moot by the extreme versatility of plants and fungi. Vegetarian meat substitutes are today often unrecognizable from their non-vegan counterparts even to the point of satisfying the craving for meat in individuals and passing for meat in blind taste tests. Though widespread adoption is still considered cost prohibitive, it should be obvious that such is a surmountable construct of the forces in this market at present. The water alone required to produce a pound of meat far exceeds the water required to produce a pound of soy. Let's not speak of the soy required to produce that same pound of meat. Maintain with me here. The nature based underpinnings of our concept of good humor manifest in the word itself. Floral is as much a synonym for good humor as verve is for energy. The ritual maintain between woman and plant or between man and plant is our single greatest keystone to unlocking the infinite possibilities of Greater Humanity and Greater Sustainability. It must be studied and applied at every step of our process including the mitigation and resourcing of waste. It should strike us as a bolt of awareness when photovoltaic energy synthesis is mastered, after all, plants enjoy a population far and away greater than our own on earth via photo-synthesis. It is true that our disastrous effects on the earth's climate were slow to come to general awareness. It is also true that a company is professing to have mastered Zero-Impact housing through a combination of recycled material, waste composting, solar energy and other considerations. Maintain with that mode of thinking. Would it clearly indicate an individual's co-empathy and humanity if she or he were to wear such a company's t-shirt? If you are interested in conveying the goodwill of a character, such can be done more effectively than an "I Heart Mom" tattoo.

Chapter 4

What's In a Name

[Name]

Liberal is a far less principled notion than its Progressive exponence. An interesting argument is that the liberal's drawback is potentially its tendency toward amelioration and not reparation. #

The Street Artist is oft assumed a champion of the Liberal political mind. But what is Liberal? Is it a decent banner for the Street Artist to fly high and march under perpetually? The term Liberal when applied to social systems is assailed by opposing minds as being socially irresponsible. #

Liberals want a strip-joint in every neighborhood and promise free beer for all... who are over, say, thirteen. That is a great caricature from the opposing mind. It's a relatively standard formula, bear in mind 'free beer' is not the liberal folly they hope to exaggerate. The opposing mind himself, in the arena of politics, may offer 'free sunday school' for all people... over, say, 8 months old. It's the beer. The exploitation of populist beer affinity is his platform leak and a window to his character flaws. Just so. #

Is this a just accusation (if unabideably exaggerated)? When a word is taken on for the purposes of identification, linguistics continue to exert influence on it. The people who elect to be identified with that word will have the complex system of language guiding all they proclaim and all that is claimed regarding that identification. #

'Liberty' gives us an opportunity to have a bit of semantic indulgence when applying it to social systems. Keep in mind, it is *need* that determined where a conjugation ultimately manifested its definition. Language evolves as social relations/social systems evolve thus the linguist is often using language as a predicate to understanding and perhaps even inferring future manifestations of popular objectives and identifications. #

Previous usage, prior to personal or group identification is the most direct officiation. The previous usage of other conjugations is not far behind. They are linesmen, if you will. In the case of conjugations where previous usage is of scarce reference the 'linesmen' must officiate directly. Only names and prospired words are free from referees and must rely on the audience reaction to determine who is scoring higher or faring better. An audience composed of self-important synonyms, aggressive homonyms and everyone else. #

If a doctor tells you to liberally apply a cream to your rash at prescribed intervals, his usage of and your understanding of the word 'liberal' is important to your very survival. He obviously wants you to keep mind of the time and use enough at the appropriate time. Does he want you to break it out like anarchy and slap it on zealously? No more than he wants you to liberally shrug and use none. #

The Liberal mind urges along the incremental mode of 'enough': enough, rather than too little. The dicremental mode of 'enough' being: 'stop, that's enough.' The aforementioned tendency is specific to things it sees as positive for people and for a social system. So the "exploitation of populist beer affinity" is a bit zealous as accusations go. #

How might the Liberal be corralled to its actual faults using the system of language to force a certain abandonment of identifying banner in order to fare well in debate? It's important to note its origin in the Latin word Libris i.e. Books. Shall we accuse him of Libel, acting like a Librarian, or acting like a Libertine? When you were new to libraries the Librarian spent much time in the dicremental mode of enough (Shh). As you are now obsessed with Wireless Fidelity, the Librarian spends her energy encouraging you to source incrementally and not just rely on Wikipedia. #

Two questions. That first Librarian... Libertarian? Okay, the better question. Do conjugations careen back and forth in connotation as you sequence through them from shortest to longest/longest to shortest? The second question *is* more interesting, but mostly hypothetical. (The first question is just ironclad truth.) Especially when dealing with social systems, the affinity for chosen words and the counter-affinity of the opposing mind makes the dynamic divergence of connotative relations an observable reality. #

When it comes to popular objectives and identifications, flexibility is a greater asset than rigidity. Incremental and dicremental notion on a kind of flexibility. A malleable metal that can be pulled into wire has greater resolve than a viscous drop of saliva that can be pulled into a threadlike stream. For a question in the mode of 'How much do we give?' Even an ambiguous incremental/dicremental concept of 'enough [shrug]' has greater resolve than 'have it your way'. #

A useful example of fluidity making superior defense at a given time, the Progressivist might be more useful to the present social systems than Progressives who are countered with accusations of moral ambivalence. Progressivism as a word is innately rooted in purpose and offers a counter-narrative to stagnation and resistance to progress. The Progressive on the other hand, just sounds like he's going somewhere. #

Is moral ambivalence an Achilles heel to the progressive mentality? It's certainly less detrimental than the notion of moral bankruptcy. But social Change is reliant on a very present sense of moral integrity. #

If we engage progressive values with proactive and resolved ambition, would supposed ambivalence give way to Progressivism? #

When utilizing the phrase Civil Servant to refer to our community organizers, politicians, and the like we often demote the nature of their influence which isn't all strange considering the nature of constituent. However, a directing mind retains and maintains a significant amount of influence. It is deeded to that official or co-operator as per the evidence of their loyalty and integrity. In television production as in motion picture for cinema, directors are an integral part. However, the TV director isn't regarded quite nearly as a visionary part of the final product as the motion picture director. They are often interchanged within the run of a singular season of a singular series. Therein, the Director begins to incontrovertibly resemble the Civil Servant. #

When it comes to art forms that provide example, critique and/or parallel of our Social Systems, flexibility becomes a great asset of the Directing mind. Rigidity may well be a present and pronounced social ill thus manifest in socially intra-active art, but it doesn't command focus in analysis for understanding and replication. Lets discard the notion of rigidity in this body of art and replace it with a fair amount of predictability, or more appropriately co-empathy. Therein distinguishing it yet an asset to the directing mind or minds. #

Overseeing the Creative Direction of a project is invariably being responsible for the cohesion of contributions from a great number of artist, subjects or contributors. #

The Subject is not just a contributor like a Set Dresser. The Subject is not just a performer. The Subject may require both an artist and a performer within the very same project. The Subject may require a performer who is an artist in addition to the aforementioned artist required. For example, a Subject I incorporate might require both an illustrator and a performer who is a martial artist. The "Subject" we speak of is 'Character en Generation'. #

Social Systems can be as vast as an industry or inter-governmental policy; as inevitable as a community or local-organizing system; or as overlooked as a communicative application or group athletic-endeavor. #

Regarding the "potentially overlooked" examples (and there are an infinity more), we mentioned previously in Chapter 1 the malleability of 'communicative application' as it can be replicated in ever changing mode and ever evolving medium. All of the aforementioned examples were superlative in their utility on scales massively reductive per interval. Much like the interval between the Model UN and the actual United Nations is massively reduced to fit within a student body. #

The group-athletic endeavor is the most dynamic and utile small-scale Social System for the analysis and replication of human interaction via microcosmic comparison. Furthermore, we can immediately expand the scrimmage into a match, a tournament, a conference, a league and maintain various dynamic understandings even as a phalanx of social system builds before our eyes. #

The utility and dynamicity of group-athletic-endeavor as microcosm of social systematics (and indeed as the manifest duality of macro-cosmic social systematics) can be explored further in a work more aptly titled *Creative Direction*. #

Such utility of group-athletic-endeavor applies to dynamics as rudimentary as the tendency of an individual when interacting in exclusive with another individual. Position A of Team A may meet Position A of Team B in the coffee shop where p.A/t.A is barista and p.A/t.B is a customer. There is no need for macro-cosmic or microcosmic understanding. What we have is auxiliary understanding of the individuals that can be further refined through the generation of character. #

We can use an exemplary social system of group athletics to further develop the Subjects without letting assumed inclination assume the mantle of surrogate decision maker. Here I will refine our understanding within our presumably democratic inclinations: Position A is Team Captain. #

The various duties within an athletic team contain dynamic tendencies that are recognizable and can be translated to other forms of social interaction. In *Creative Direction* I might well spend an elongated time on the analogical 'Teaming' of Subjects with a uniting investment and how this might seemingly automate the finer points of some natural interactions, freeing us up to focus on the Creative Direction of a greater whole. #

Here in *Character Generation* let me point out that individual identifications/objectives and group identifications/objectives are as indispensable to the Street Artist Method as Subject is indispensable to Direction. One can Direct a work of visual motion/storytelling without a Subject, yet the audience or the director of photography invariably assumes the mantle/perspective of Subject. The Street Artist method too can be engaged counter to convention in terms of Character as we generally know it. And you don't have to go as far as putting your audience in the shoes of a Street Artist. But if you do, call me. #

One can complete the process of Character Generation without ever providing the Subject a "Name". #

A Subject's 'traits' and 'aptitudes' can manifest fairly clearly in their subscription to popular identifications and objectives. This can be their global citizenhood or the more specific citizenship they claim to a Nation, it can be political leanings even those rarely identified with a political party a la feminist or venture capitalist. It can be their profession, hobby, position in a family or organization. It can be their fraternity or sorority to an arbitrary fanaticism. In-exhaustive examples. #

Names, like prospired words, can serve to refine a Subject's character without being the Subject's handle or 'personal name of reference'. The media in the 2010s has been having a field day with group identifications re popular music acts. The pop stars are participant, and together they have gleefully bastardized the conventions of conjugation to suit the needs of their references in common. It's been done elsewhere. The life-coach who customizes his curriculum to your chosen idol calls himself a Modeler not to be confused with Model. In the same way, fans of a prominent singing group have been dubbed Directioners not to be confused with aspiring Directors with a long way to go. #

Where conjugations are elaborative as such, Names and prospired words intend to be originative in their refining of a Subject's character (read: people rep their set). They can be applied to the useful referencing of a Subject's traits and aptitudes via her/his subscription to individual or group identifications/objectives. #

If you endeavor to use athletic social systems in Character Generation or Creative Direction, or if you have athletic social systems within your socially intra-active body of art; you may encounter a hybridization of prospirancy in relation to words.

Phonetics imbue words with varying sensations and connotations. The aspirance to the most sentient phonetic emulations within a given language is a distinction of interpersonal nomenclature. We refuse to settle for less when naming our brethren. We are loathe to settle for less when naming out teams. #

The referees of "conjugation" are predisposed. It is left up to us. If I return to the earlier example and tell you Barista Captain of Team Green is greeting and serving Customer Captain of The Couriaz, our auxiliary understanding of the individuals has been yet refined. With a modest understanding of their commonalities and of the intensity of their rivalry, we can make a pseudo-democratic ascertainment as to whether the encounter will be uneventful, entertaining, enlightening, or game-changing. #

Make an uninvolved assumption about the encounter between p.A/t.A and p.A/t.B. At a minimum, guess which of the four aforementioned categories it will fall into. Would your assumption be different if it were instead the Green Team and the Couriers? The syntax of Team A invites more connotations than merely the standard definition of 'Green'. The phonetics of Team B imbue it with a sense of smoothness and flourish whereas the standard spelling is laden with sensations of hurry or haste manifest in the doubled usage of 'R'. #

We can go further with our analysis. Couriers has a subconscious divide between U and R in a mental effort to create phonetic sub-words that exist without sharing letters, one of several natural inclinations. This is far inferior to the phonetic sub-word divide between R and I in Couriaz that preserves the inter-linguistically meaningful root 'Cour' whereas the alternative fixates on 'Cou' and exasperates a sense of archaicness. Those divides are gleaned by carefully considering how we stress syllables in a particular language. #

When we allow for the sharing of letters between phonetic sub-words, 'riaz' proves more useful to our auxiliary understanding of individuals identified by the team of reference. It is imbued with sensations and connotations of upward movement and of light. These kind of subwords are a visual reflex in most readers. #

Athletic Social Systems are by no means the only place where you may encounter an inclination toward prospirence in relation to identification. Neither are baby names, nick names, ghetto names, gangster names, pet names (human) and pet names (animal) etc. #

The aspirance to the most sentient phonetic emulations within a given language is a distinction of interpersonal nomenclature. #

Interpersonal nomenclature should, for the most part, be considered distinct from scientific nomenclature. That being as it is, it absolutely encompasses 'commercial name generation'. Thus extending to Business names, Product names, Establishment names, Venue names, Vessel names, District/Neighborhood names etc. They are prospired by individuals to aide in interpersonal communication between the entity and its commercial base. #

The information age has furthermore encouraged the embrace of titular prospirancy by entrepreneurs even to an outlandish degree. As it was believed an industry built on revolutionary infrastructure mandated outstanding even outlandish recognizability and to normalize the oddity was a feat of and a testament to the business model of reference. Business is no stranger to the need for conjunctive and/or distinctive originality in titular heading. The Editor at Large simply couldn't occupy the Editor in Chief mold, the Social Media Intern required recognition beyond usual internhood, the Fashionista couldn't settle for being merely a Stylist, and the Creative... was fortunately not the Procreative since they're clearly averse to commitment. #

The Creative can well be considered a conjunctive prospirence. Perhaps Creative Director was hacked in half thus freeing the former overseer to "do whatever". Or perhaps the Creator made a distinct break from his prime time TV style idolatry and ceded a few ounces of creative control to his writers, remaining thus Creative. It is my understanding that the Creative works well in a low-manpower endeavor perhaps functioning as the relateable end of a duo made whole by his partner, Programmer. #

Do not neglect the fact that Conjugation, especially wherein identifications and objectives come into play, is not exclusive to verbs (and I will spend no time whatsoever branding words as certain "parts of speech"); But more richly and relevantly, Conjugation is not exclusive to suffixial changes, it applies to prefixial amendments as well. #

One such prefixial conjugation that furthermore is an example of aspirance to the most sentient phonetic emulations within a given language is Parasamaraton. As prefixes go, 'para' is both consistently beautiful and widely neglected. The popularity and decline of the term Supernatural is an example of that neglect in action. Things that were Above/Beyond/Outside of Nature or our Natural World occurred and were supported with evidence of their occurrence. What were they then? Neonatural? Or was there a non-natural world of nature we should pay heed? #

Para avoids those pitfalls of reasoning by refusing to assume dominance. In medicine, Para can denote a disordered faculty or function. But keep in mind in the case of disorder; there is still faculty, there is still function. Such is the case with the Paranormal. It is distinct from, but analogous to its root word. There is the acknowledgment of parallels. #

The notion of 'para' meaning subsidiary or assisting is much less frequent and can be disputed. The paramedic is one such example listed as subsidiary or assisting by reputable dictionaries. I would argue that the 'paramedic' is not para to informal medics (i.e. medical professionals) but rather para to military medics from whence they quite clearly evolved. Thus it is 'distinct from, but analogous to' the medic. Just as a paramilitary is distinct from but analogous to a military. #

The acknowledgment of parallels is as significant as the chasm between normal and paranormal is jarring. Remember, popular English needed a second "go" at that concept in order to get it right. The Paramedic is distinct from but analogous to the Medic wherein peacetime or normalcy requires a similar service as that which is provided during unrest and disruption. Similarly the Parasamaraton is prospired to be distinct from but analogous to the Samaritan wherein unrest and disruption require a similar service as that which is provided during peacetime or normalcy. #

Endeavoring a new conjugation may require prospirence on your part when taking into account the co-active and interactive nature of our phalanx of Social Systems. The proposed Hyperloop system is neither plane or train nor automobile. It is in fact 'loop'. A high-speed loop. It may hopefully offset carmageddon which is a periodic logistical failure that deceases the utility of automobiles by way of traffic quagmire. #

Why not Phenomenaloop? They even share three letters. Hyper-speed is literal and takes precedence over awesomeness during conveyance. Why not autopocalypse? Well, those who coined the phrase gave concerted thought to the fact that cars with single occupants were the problem. More bus traffic and van traffic would in fact reduce the traffic jam when properly utilized. Automobiles in general were not to blame. Don't quote me. #

You might never suspect that the suffix on the word Principal is indicative of its place in a social system. You might realize it after encountering the Basque healer Erapal, or the Indian earth protector Mahipal. 'Pal' is indeed the mark of a Protector. #

That is not unlike the reasoning behind the alteration of the spelling of the root Samaritan in its analogous other. What we know about the need for Parasamaratons is that they are considered part and parcel to the Public Service Sector and additionally market Public Personas not unlike a politician. They can be of non-governmental-organizations or not-for-profit organizations but most importantly they should champion a specific civil body who should as well have some oversight as to how the time and resources are used in serving them. They should, in effect, have a constituent. 'Ton' is indeed the mark of a Champion. #

Final paragraph:

Approach this facet of your character with an open mind. As your character moves from place to place in the verse, they will encounter different characters with different ways of pronouncing things. Convey the name with the character's language in mind and be aware of the instinctual inflections others may put on it and how that minutely alters the impression the name gives. Share the name as accurately as possible and encourage your audience to learn how it sounds when it is spoken. Additional clarity can be provided with informal names, calls or easy to convey characteristics. If a character is allowed to perform without a name your audience will have a tendency to construe one for the sake of their discussion of your art. Easy to convey characteristics often find their way into those informal names. I'll do a thing like that periodically because it is good practice when generating character. It is not unlike the Working Title. Isn't that true, Voracious Reader?

Chapter 5

Vandalism

[Vandalism]

The instinctual inclination toward self identification manifests beyond the way an individual alters their outward appearance. It manifests beyond the way an individual maintains their interpersonal behaviors. Behavioral habits, traits, and other individualization of phenotypical norms do not stop there. Self identification manifests in the way people maintain their interrelational behaviors as well. #

Self Identification is not limited to manifestations of the physical form or vocally conveyed self projection. Two facets of self identification involve the deliberate impressions individuals leave on their environment and on other individuals. #

Deliberate impressions on our environment and subsequently other people is the evolutionary root of Art and Street Art. #

Hair & makeup artistry, tattooing & piercing, and garment design notwithstanding; we do not isolate and analyze the individual's direct impression on the bodies of other individuals in this text. Perhaps Chiropractory or some other dark art. With these facets of self identification we will include relevant forms with our hyper-relevant potentially *autonomous* acts and contributions. Those mentioned above have potential duality. Deliberate impressions on our bodies to subsequently impress upon the minds of other people are a category of art we refer to in Chapter 9: 'The Marks of Passage'. #

Street Art has the distinction of being even more intrinsic to an individual's artistic inclination to separate self from environment.

Those who describe this as a need are somewhat incorrect. It is not a 'need'. It is an Evolution. At its core, Street Art iterates that point nearly as directly as the earliest forms of human art. #

As we refer to environment here, we encompass both an individual's natural surroundings and their structural surroundings. As human beings, we gravitate toward structure even in our natural environment. #

Let me spend only that much time dancing about architecture as they say. Gravitating toward structure is only one connotation for the tendency toward order. When immersing ourselves into social interaction and dividing our time between social systems, different cultures give varying degrees of credence to different social tendencies within our social systems. #

When we convene the primary objectives of a given day, more often than not, circulation of ideas and concepts is a necessary directive. The act of merely passing a single object from one individual and his extended social interaction, to another individual with an extended social interaction of his own, can involve a number of modal considerations. #

Proximity has been one of Humanity's earliest considerations and much time in history has been spent dancing about architecture. Keep in mind that 'about' in this and many cases incorporates both 'within' and 'without'. #

Cities in many parts of the world, are newly grappling with the urgency for legislation to determine what kind of signs can go in what areas and what signs to ban. LED technology has greatly affected the ability to catch the eye with a minimally conductive infrastructure. Minimally internally conductive; as in less potentially combustible nor with the heightened ability to short-out and have its recognizability immediately depleted. #

It has not proven to be the product/service nor the signage but the general popularity of a thoroughfare that has required the stoppage of all promotional amendments. This signage-stoppage is contingent on literal Legislation before it can reconvene because there is danger in distracting people so thoroughly on a path of irrelevate popularity. #

The dangers of distraction are an issue behooving legality– not just the visual word-recognition diversion of attention, but as well the kinds of responses intended as well as the kinds of responses elicited without intent. #

Unforeseen decreases in speed can cause dangerous traffic conditions. Stopping and stalling can also cause dangerous conditions even in a pedestrian-only plaza. #

The kind of responses intended and the kind of responses elicited without intent can be a part of the legal basis for distinguishing between vandalism and Street Art. #

A popular jest in street art culture, often attributed to the Collective that popularized Stencil Graffiti in the mainstream, says that getting forgiveness is easier than getting permission. #

Vandalism refers to marks and changes made to the appearance of a publicly or privately visible piece of property with the intention of defacing the object. Vandalism is often intended to affect the integrity of an object and can lead to degradation or even the collapse of habitable structures. #

Commercial advertisement is rarely composed in the general or immediately recognizable modalities of Street Art. However, an oppositional is true. Street Art frequently is composed directly utilizing the varying standards of advertismal design. #

Wherein vandalism takes particular care not to have an effect on the integrity of an object, it strays exceptionally close to the Street Arts of Mural and Installation. Bear in mind, installation art can be as simply executed as a light based projection onto a visible surface. #

I've recently had the cyber-discussion with a few thousand of my phantom constituent as to the acclimating of one's public persona and art into the service of a Social Purpose beyond art or into the service of Social Justice. It requires one thing. Practice. #

Bear in mind we have defined installation art as *unlikely* to damage the integrity of an object. Yet, when we consider the word installation we automatically tend to consider mechanical fastening and annexing. So, with a vague and elementary example imagined in our minds, we can assume practice alone will not make you successful in Installation Art, which can benefit from a certain degree of inanonymity. Let alone in social purpose/justice which are appreciative of the benefits of inanonymity. Effective Practice requires one thing. Study. #

The installation of a work involving a light based projection onto a surface has been used of late with Social Purpose/Justice in mind. One formidable example was to protest working conditions in sweat-shops and the blind profiteering that surrounds it. Another was the presentation of musical motion picture shorts in unusual public locations. This was accompanied by a mass distribution model likely based on one pioneered by a public radio figure as well recently. It was also accompanied by promotion likely based on a model phased into common knowledge through groups of engagors connected by mobile devices. #

The method of promoting an event within hours of its intended occurrence through group texting and mass messaging services is commonly known as the Flash Mob. In its infancy, flash mobs were not particularly serious in nature. They came across as a challenge or game to see if an unusual amount of people could suddenly converge on a location often bearing a uniform and unusual object. #

The social purpose/social justice applications of the flash mob manifested to most during its perpetual utilization and are forthcoming. Given the penchant of governing bodies to obstruct peaceful demonstration that is at odds with their interests by demanding bureaucratic permits, setting curfews, and outright banning demonstration; the flash mob is an empowering expression of the Right To Peacefully Assemble. #

When an installation takes special care to avoid permanently altering supporting structures, artistry is inherent in the contrast between the performance art piece and the way the structure normally appears. Preserving the art that is evident in performance/production of an installation can yet be done in a number of ways. Videography is a common one. Choreography happens to be one as well. Choreography of coordination has the distinct benefit of facilitating reproduction of any enduring artwork. #

When producing art for public spaces, the time set aside for the production of the artwork is often inconducive to performance and certain performance art. To avoid incursions of the public into the work in progress, various considerations are taken. The artistic value of the linear production of the art is entirely up to the artist at work. Keep in mind those considerations are also taken if producing the art away from areas where it will later be displayed (perhaps with the flourish of seasoned performance artist or practiced coordinated installation artist). #

The contrast between the usual appearance of a performance space, venue, or display can be maximized for artistic effect if the space changes little otherwise. This is more the case for art than for performance. Though the conjunction of the two can fare well in artistic spaces and performance spaces, the latter of which would host other performances more frequently. Keep in mind if a performance space hosts a homogeneity of productions, your performance or performance art could very well utilize the contrast between itself and the usual to leave an artistic impression on the observer. #

In Street Art, the "artistic space" varies almost endlessly. Installation art often resembles a performance art piece in the preciseness of the reintroduction technique. Installation, in the very nature of the word, connotes coordination and expertise.

There is a form of installation art that occupies the region between temporary audio/visual experiences and corporate industrial art. #

In 1977 a group of Feminist artist raised millions to fight a bill introduced by a California state senator to ban lesbian and gay teachers from public schools. This was immediately following what is possibly the first anti-gay rights ordinance passed in the U.S. in Florida. Resistance was waged in part with an installation art piece that incorporated performance art. In all reality, it incorporated and invited the audience to participate in the performance art. An entire second-hand store or thrift store was installed in an artistic space where the persecuted academics would present their identity-affirming performance pieces to the audience in what was designed to feel very much like a real and casual encounter. Donations of goods "to the store" were encouraged and the movement became prominent in popular media eventually raising huge sums. #

The installation of the store above involves a process very similar to the way an Art Director functions on a movie set. Unlike a film set where the risk of non-sequitur manifesting in the finished film puts the art director in charge of a "Hot Set" (one that should be carefully maintained in appearance), the feminist thrift store required the artistic participation of the audience in the wholistic intent of involving community in holding lawmakers accountable. #

The law and litigation are inevitably a prime point of focus when considering the artistic value of 2D visual-medium vandalism in its basic and artistically evolved forms. It presently reaches all the way back to the origins of ancestral human vandal art as there is the concern that such manifestations, for example cave paintings in Botswana, should be protected by law and proceeds from the showing of the artwork should go to benefit the local and indigenous community. Such manifestations are very often today deemed World Heritage Sites. #

Today, the creation of wall paintings on structures has a number of legalities to consider. Litigation has ensued in Long Island City where a vacant building lot of cult-status and infamy was recently turned over to developers and Street Artist who were for a long time allowed to render and display their artwork there took issue with not being allowed to remove their artwork from the premises before renovation. [Update: as I am editing this for the first print edition, the Artist have won a judgement in excess of 6 million dollars.] #

This is not a casual oversight. Evidenced by another case where my early mentor the poet and blind proprietor of a Lower East Side gallery and community center, in turning his building over to encroaching developers, had his walls scrawled with "All Art Must Go" before the parting festivities resulting in the organization members removing a large chunk of the building's wall that had been hand painted by an internationally renowned Art Superstar. Thus preserving a centerpiece of the artwork and rendering any attempted exploitation by the shrewd and wily new owners prime for ridicule and even charges of Misappropriation of Intellectual Property and Grand Larceny through Fraudulent Deception. #

Litigation has ensued most obviously where a Street Artist creates a piece on a structure without the solicitation or consent of the property owner. Graffiti art circles are a maze of anonymity and code names for that reason, even today as the art form has evolved into the public sphere and global respectability. There are numerous cases of an artist' Tag, or stylized signature, being used to prosecute them in the late 70s, early 80's and beyond. #

At some interval of time, it was doubtlessly a "golden parachute" for an Artist to take responsibility for his or her work often done in abandoned or unused tax-payer owned spaces. Fines were often surmountable especially with the renown and credibility that came with media attention and recognizability. Artfulness was the inextricable requisite. Social Purpose often played a role in the selecting of tax-payer owned, neglected property. Artfulness treads the tightrope of commanding attention, building intrigue, and capitalizing on timely de-anonymity. Yet the risk is real, as Jail is not unheard of by any stretch of the imagination. #

Hip hop is not alone as a subcultural phenomenon that enshrined Street Art into its doctrine and aided in its legitimization in the eyes of the unfamiliar. Punk Rock, whose influence can still be seen in the Antifa movement gaining global popularity, has done the same. Certain forms of Print Art reached a crescendo of Art World acceptance in the 1970s. It would be enough to force exclusion of Print Art discussion when discussing Street Art. However Punk Rock long incorporated Print Art into its promotion of ideas and events, and often did so through the Street Art technique of Wheatpaste. #

Take note here: Illicit Street Artwork enjoys the same Copyright protection as legal and commissioned Street Artwork. Fixation for an observable period of time and Originality are the requisites of copyright protection for Mural, Graffiti Mural and Wheatpaste Mural artwork. #

Litigation has arisen most recently as artist have found their Copyrights infringed upon by vendors selling memorabilia, prints, and other items bearing the work of Graffiti artist. There is a casual assumption that Street Artist will not prosecute, either because of a moral code or a lack of resources to do so. As it is that known Street Artist are among the most widely recognized names and styles in the contemporary art world, that assumption is a dangerous one to make. #

When successful graffiti artist who began their craft in the 80s engaged the U.S. Copyright Office, they often did so via poor-man's-copyright; photographed works sealed, postmarked, and mailed to self. This was before the advent of the internet and the Street Artist protocol of publishing new artworks to a personal blog (even if password privatized) or a personal website thus effectively copyrighting the work. One thing remains the same, encouraging the action falls in perfect line with the difficulty of young artist and Street Artist to by happenstance have the resources to protect their work. #

The photo-sharing application we allude to in Chapter 1: 'The Phantom Constituent', is said to be democratizing art. The headline posing that question, rhetorically, appeared after a relatively affluent individual was caught and prosecuted for selling the artwork of others, simply lifted from the site, for hundreds of thousands of dollars verging on literal millions. #

Litigation arises in strange ways too concerning art with its roots in Vandalism. Recently a Queens NY city councilman introduced a proposal to ban stores from selling a form of Spray Chalk that is marketed to adolescents. This is a product that is essentially calcium carbonate and like any other chalk it washes off when it rains. His argument was that the spray mechanism for application mimics/encourages graffiti vandalism and acts as an, I suppose "gateway utensil" to a life of criminal vandalism. #

His proposal was rejected on the very simple grounds that lawmakers agreed they had no ability or invective to ban a perfectly legal product for its aesthetic attributes and usability design considerations. My memory presents this to me as the city councilman before a particular court, and if that is the case it was in fact the Judiciary that asserted a lack of directive or initiative. Better luck next time, anti-chalk-art crusader. #

Final Paragraph:

Consider the way action heroes are romanticized once they happen to be chronic samaritans. The consumer penchant for idolizing a hero's suaveness and comandingness of presence is rooted somewhere. The ability to pull off daunting acrobatics and valiant interceptions is not particularly material to the intensive portrayal of a character who does a lot of good in the world. It is, to the keen observer, a liability and a sign of a character's innate recklessness but it has for some reason become the centerpiece of our observation of "Heroes". There is in that promulgation part of the same inclination that drove the advent of the sport Parkour. Parkour involves performing daunting acrobatics in urban environments. It is primarily athletic performance, but it can on occasion be considered performance art. The spiritual and social validation of mastering chance and pomp are internal drives that people have grown to view as part and parcel to the notion of being a hero. There's an evolution of that drive present when people play as a specific character in a video game or root for an action hero in a movie. This version furthermore incorporates the age-old desire to have immediate and dramatic effect over one's physical environment. Navigating the realistic constraints of a video game are greatly and subconsciously rewarded by moments when a character is able to, for example, eliminate an entire wall. Vandalism is not Demolition. The propensity for vandalism should be considered as a reasonably healthy character attribute intended to mitigate and artistically manifest the deep-seated human desire to alter their physical environment dramatically without exhausting effort. And if you happen to find a hero's consistency and diligent, deliberate effort to be worthy of examination and entertaining on a deeper level; his or her penchant for, say, ripping out and pocketing a page from a riveting text, is an exemplary method for touching the minds of those who would love to be Heroes but are still confined to the stereotypical ideals of recklessness.

Chapter 6

Accessory to Utility

[Utility]

Hard object theory is a study of utility. Hardness as it relates to utility here can also refer to the difficulty of the task. The "object" of one's actions, if you will. In the case of utensils and tools, and as well instruments and devices, finding the right one for the task may likewise be considered difficult or hard. Applications and even complex software can fall within the bounds of Hard object theory. #

Accessory to utility is scenario oriented study: Successful utilization of an object wherein the catalyst for use comes from without of the primary subject. When Character Development and Character Creation inform one and other, tendencies toward accessory can be elaborated to the point of a personality's defining utilities. These tendencies manifest less frequently than most interpersonal tendencies and many interrelational tendencies. Indeed less frequent than your average habit. But they go a long way toward helping define a character. #

Street Art is often spontaneous. It is often elaborately premeditated. It is often produced as a live installation. #

A tool, utensil, instrument, or device that helps define a character will generally be portable. A novel character I can describe to you requires another personality entirely to physically maintain a defining object. What we've termed the 'Man on the Street' performance artist requires what we generally call a DP which is a camera operator or videographer adept in on-location directing. #

The 'DP' or 'Director of Photography' is more often than not adept in on-location directing to the point of requiring no additional Directors or to herself/himself directing additional camera operators. The nature of photography has evolved to occur frequently outside of a studio or set. A massively relevant part of photography's evolution was its transition to Street Art. #

The still-motion photographer is an iconic Street Artist. Few have not seen one in action and few could not mimic the posture and motion of a 'Street Photographer' in action. Motion photographers and videographers can be similarly distinct. Their formidability as Street Artist is less established mostly due to the lack of a consummate mode of street filmmaking or street videography. Albeit music video incorporating street montage is as frequent if not more frequent than (e.g.) Man on the Street performance art. #

The portability of a defining object in Character Generation is necessitated by the desire that the object be readily available to the character and seen frequently enough with the character to become a visual characteristic of casual or intensive recognition. #

The utility of a defining object generally needs to meet a criteria of indispensability or relative frequency. An interrelational or interpersonal tendency encompasses even the most basic physical tic or verbal idiosyncrasy. Thus 'frequency' in terms of a 'tendency toward utility' is a relative term. One of the most frequent Accessory to Utility manifestations, by both frequency of manifestation and frequency of use, is the rider propelled or motor driven bike or bicycle. #

Size distinction in this particular study of Character Generation is limited to objects that do not obscure the casual or intensive recognition of a character. #

The core tenets of Hard object theory include the versatility of objects. If one were to assume that large object theory was an indulgence of those tasked with studying logistics and militarism, one can argue that hard object theory incidentally encompasses practices and processes intended or used to defy or disrupt traditional logistics and its aggrandizing ethic. Personal defense, martial art, espionage, and cyber-espionage are such areas. #

Suffice to say the most intrinsic and most easily recognized duality of a defining object is as a tool of self-defense. A formidable example that elaborates the parameters of versatility where character generation is concerned is the 'Intuitionist'. Introduced into modern literature via a novel bearing the same name, the intuitionist is an elevator inspector who relies heavily on sensation when engaging the particular vessel, mechanisms, and system they are inspecting. #

Versatility where character generation is concerned is not limited to dualities or multiplicities of use for a defining object. The way an object is transported is a facet of its versatility. The standardized screwdriver issued to the inspector by the inspection agency for the removing and replacing of inspection certificates emplaced in an elevator is a defining object of the intuitionist. It is a canny example of an object that occupies the manifest core of Hard object theory countering traditional logistical thinking with its most obvious versatility. #

From a simplified perspective, Hard object theory is a brain training exercise in self-defense. It eschews projectile, ballistic, and thermodynamic objects not only for their disconnection of component/continence, but for the liability of their unchecked trajectories when in use. In its complexial form it advances to hardware, and applications thereof, that are definitively precise when utilized. Accessory to Utility is further study of the Complexial features of Hard object theory. Complexial refers to attributes that are invariant under scenario application (or isomorphic comparison/transformation). #

Note that our modern definition of "Hardware and Applications thereof" varies widely from socket wrenches to remote climate control. Our guideline remains the same 'The successful utilization of an object wherein the catalyst for use comes from without of the primary subject.' That is "in and of itself" the invariant attribute of Hard object theory in complexial study. Just like the core melody in a set of covers of the same song, the aforementioned is an attribute that is consistent between all complexes in a set of isomorphic complexes. #

We analyze scenarios independently of one another as well. That is the isolation and observation of variants that 'isomorphic' denotes. If a Street Artist were tasked with procuring a self-conceived, candid photograph of Sam Cooke having an intimate conversation, Accessory to Utility is concerned with the invariant attributes of that endeavor: Mr. Cooke, the catalyst, will manifest; demi-logistical considerations will be taken; the photograph will be procured. Success. The defining Accessory to Utility of the scenario, however, may vary and should be taken into careful consideration when elaborating the utility of a character. #

The Street Photographer may be very well defined and differentiated from busybodies or profiteering photogs in her or his mannerism and may need be additionally defined by no other object than his or her camera. The Installation Artist who hopes to project fresh and familiar romantic images over the chosen personality as said personality chats before the inconspicuous facade of an intended mural thus getting a picture of Mr. Cook emitting thought bubbles that will eventually seem to transform the wall, however may not fare as well. His unfamiliarity with the casual grace of Street Photographers may leave him slapped upside the head. #

Demi-logistical consideration as such is where scenario can inform Character Generation via Accessory to Utility. The Installation Artist may want to use haste to differentiate themself from the busybodies and profiteering photogs that suffer Mr. Cooke's occasionally physical admonition. Haste is a tenuous additive to such scenarios because people react to *it* as well. They may react and ruin the intended candidness or romance of the photograph. That is itself a better result than a reaction that is reflexive/defensive/aggressive toward haste and results in injury to the photographer, or detention by the law for presenting oneself as a credible threat. #

The previously described reaction has a similar reason to why bedding down to wait with telescopic observational and photographic equipment is simplex and problematic. An entire apartment building can come under the immediate scrutiny of the law in force if a single individual is noticed presenting a credible threat. Mr. Cooke has the right to privacy. In allowing an Artist to successfully complete the task at hand, Sam is balancing the marketing of a Public Persona by allowing for occasional intrusion into his private life so long as it is a public place that he has chosen to have the private conversation. #

One might make the demi-logistical consideration to wear in-line skates in order to differentiate themselves from busybodies and profiteers. Such skates would have the benefit of making haste into a more amusing spectacle and tempering the subjects eventual reaction. For scenarios such as this where the Catalyst is a human being, such methods of accelerating one's pace are preferable to motor driven transport and even pedal powered bikes. Cars and like vehicles fail the 'obscuring the character' rule of Accessory to Utility. Bicycles require intensive motor attention from the rider and are accident prone if multitasking comes into their function. #

Once an object like in-line skates fulfills the complexial features of an Accessory to Utility scenario, it is the responsibility of a creative director to furthermore apply it over and over in various isomorphic complexes to determine the versatility of its utility and subsequently the frequency and prominence of its manifestation with or in-the-possession-of a specific character. #

If you are concerned with the qualifications of a Vespa as accessory, be aware of the syntactic ambiguity of Accessory to Utility. The scenario orientation of the study dictates that the primary character of any example is themselves an Accessory. In the way that an Accessory to a strong-arm robbery plays lookout while the suspect roughs up the clerk. This may be crude and insulting to the Character Generation novice considering that bringing your puppy to distract and enamor Mr. Cooke violates the parameters of 'Object'. Meanwhile you are an Accessory. That's life. #

While we've isolated the word Accessory, let us touch on another one of the most common manifestations of Accessory to Utility and observe the way it applies to simplicial Hard object theory. Procuring, toting, obscuring and like notions are often motive actions of a scenario or task. The most obvious manifestation of those basic inevitabilities would surely be easy to obscure (versatility) as we instead regard (admire) its greater (really) complex character. #

The 'Woman about Town' can generally be considered a complex character. If you are still disaffected that we reduced you to accessory earlier, know that reducing you to accessory is prime directive in the Woman about Town's operations. If you should step out of line (i.e. aim to abuse her) she has your allusory object in multiple sizes. Strapped and unstrapped. Get it? Reducing you to accessory? She'll generally only carry one handbag at a time if I'm making it sound like entrapment, relax. #

I am happy to identify myself as an Artist and as well as a Journalist/Writer. I would shorten it to Artist and Scribe because I definitely like the sound of that, but considering my concentration on Street Art, my oratorical poet can not play back-seat to a scribe indefinitely. #

Journalism is not unlike the work I am putting forth in this volume. It is the form of narrative argument that is specifically non-fiction and generally 'periodical' in nature. It should come as no surprise that a relevant number of Journalist are, as well, artist. I believe the Photographer Journalist can have a hard time choosing between photog and photo-journalist informally. Simply 'Journo' is better than both, informally, and they are all better than photog-journo. See Chapter 4: 'What's in a Name' for the reasons behind that. #

The media ninja is a Street Journalist. As it is that Journalism is not academically an Artistic discipline, I don't have to spend much time elaborating on that casual ascending handle or its origins. It does, for the most part, parallel the way that Street Art is different from 'Art' taken as a simplice defining matrix. #

The 'Media Ninja' makes an extra effort to appear as a working Journalistic Professional. It is imperative when immersed in unorthodox sociopolitical scenarios to be identifiably a Working Journalistic Professional. It is imperative to be identifiably so before ever the need to present identification. Unorthodox sociopolitical scenarios are inherently dangerous. A great deal of these scenarios, however, have rigorous rules and rites to their manifestation-in-prominence and additionally have media permissions protected by law. #

The backpack is popular with the media ninja and the young journalistic associations where they have phased into the common consciousness. As are hand-held video recording devices. These are objects that when combined with certain attire and behavior, convey that the person is a neutral media representative present to help spread awareness of the situation at hand. #

The backpack is a superlative example for a scenario oriented study. It can obviously be part and parcel to the utilization of a hand-held video recording device or numerous other things. Its versatility is evident in its portability, its objective transportability of contents, and as well its ergonomic attributes. #

Final paragraph:

Consider the study of utility we've named Hard Object Theory. Keep in mind that portability, versatility *and* utility are all inherent in it. Consider that in distinguishing Hard object theory from Kleptomania, we are establishing it as a basis for meaningful scenario oriented study. The study we have deemed Accessory to Utility is particularly useful in character generation if the character of note is an Artist. Not every artist requires a tool or utensil to create or showcase their art. Many require instruments but certainly not all. Some require devices. Some require versatile and/or portable containment devices perhaps in addition to any of the previous objects. This is very frequently the case for Street Artist. Consider that not every character you set forth to generate will be an Artist. Be careful not to undermine your character's artistic expression by refusing them the right to be an artist of a distinction yet unobserved to you. Thus if your character requires no defining object, be aware that they too may eventually study accessory to utility. If they come upon the scenario oriented study in their profession or occupation—imagine a crossing guard—their acclimation of that utility or necessity does not preclude artistry. On the contrary, it typically includes artistry. Individuals have the tendency to acclimate objects that are utile or necessary in a deliberate or practiced way. Self presentation, in the motor sense, is inherently artistic. Consistently considering a character's right to artistic expression of themselves is the duty of anyone who endeavors to generate character. A degree of originality is inherent in this. Also inherent are Study and Practice.

Chapter 7

The Performance Artist

[Performance Art]

Not every Performer is necessarily an Artist. In instances of vocal performance, recitation, illusionism etc a performer may be rendering a work with as much fidelity as possible to a previously observed incarnation. Even in the case of theatrical performance or acting for the screen, a performer may be taking such intensive instruction from a Director that artistic liberty is a moot notion. #

Not every Artist is a Performer. This is obvious. Take the Painter. No, really... Please... Take them all. Forgive my humor, painters. I have been known to paint, myself. That kind of humor may spawn from my school of thought that considers Art History most useful with all dates redacted. All pieces should be divided into the categories of 'contemporary' and 'a good minute' ago. To furthermore be honest, I have no issue with contemporary painters who are still ceaselessly devoted to their paint brushes. At the same time, Oscar-Claude Monet's reaction to the advent of color photography is sublime. Monet's early photo-realism was uncanny. His "if my services are no longer required I'm going to do WTF ever I want" era is a priceless study. #

The painter is a handy discipline through which to explain the Performance Artist. Can every Performer be a Performance Artist by taking artistic liberty in their performance? Let's hope not. #

Can every Artist be a be a Performance Artist by incorporating performance into their process? Absolutely. #

The second approach, however, is unlikely to simply be the origin of The Performance Artist. This can be corroborated by noting that the Performance Artist enjoys a reputation more easily paralleled to the first approach. Let's call it a 'fringe suspect' reputation. So not too many artist are in a rush to engage the second approach above. Monet could certainly insist he is the world's first Performance Painter because there was always some little bast*rd in the studio he couldn't get to vamoose. The incorporation of Performance into Art, to trade a bit of humor for an important point of clarity, takes a cue from the likes of the electronic music producer and (more elucidating) The Illusionist. Seamlessness is the operative word.
#

The Performance Artist, more often than not, immediately comes across as a performer and has honed their routine in an effort to cause the observer an eventual state of 'overwhelming acknowledgment' of the art therein. #

The paragraph you just read is, in my opinion, a viable contestant for 'most indispensable definition' of the involved and nearly abstract concept termed Performance Art. You might be surprised that my candidate for 'most indispensable example' doesn't seem to stem from or overly involve itself with the tenets of that definition. There is reason for that. My post-college roommate, the Street Poet who pioneered the study of Performance Poetry at NYU, once paused shortly into a very enthusiastic tale about a Performance Artist to define performance art for me with what he too considered "the perfect example":

The Artist is crawling down the street. In a Cape. #

He probably had a little mask over his eyes too and knee pads & wrist guards wouldn't hurt and would likely go well with the clothes he chose for the getup. The important thing is 'he is all-the-way crawling... all the way down the street'. #

We had a moment of concurrence right about "...obviously some type of statement on people who do those 'relay for life' things." To be clear, a statement on those who raise money or awareness for issues by getting people to pledge an agreed upon amount per increment of distance that they walk, jog, run, bike etc. #

Performance is not easy. We are not marginalizing Performers in this chapter. Obviously if a performer is an artist (e.g. musician) there is art inherent in the performance. But even if the Performer is just a Performer, "Performance" is not "Artless". #

Traditional Magicians, Comedians, Daredevils, Acrobats; all incorporate art into their performance. However, those artistic inclinations and artistic flourishes are more often than not steeped in tradition and at times even guilded. They serve to support the overall reception of the traditional Character the performer has assumed. #

'Street Magicians' employ a bit more nuance than most traditional characters. It is arguable that they have transcended into Performance Artist. The fact that Street Magicians are an archetypical Street Artist supports this. The venue of common public space is more conducive to small-scale illusionism than the theater can hope to be. Documentary evidence shows that small-scale illusionism is no less mystifying to observers than the large scale version. The nature of candidness suggests that it may be *more* so. Candidness is the Street Magician's Ace. #

One of the earliest manifestations to draw considerable appreciation to the discipline of Performance Art manifested in the north-east United States around the turn of the 20th century. The 'Escape Artist' elaborates on the Daredevil's performance of utilizing velocity and distance to test the bounds of dangerous feats. When velocity and distance are incorporated by Escape Artist they usually serve the same purpose as other 'impending factors' the artist uses to time their performance and to create tension/anticipation. Chief among these are 'obstruction of respiration' and 'conflagration of performance aides'. Distance and velocity have been used similarly by the Escape Artist in the form of 'impending collision'. The Escape Artist's performance generally involves freeing themselves from restraining, restrictive, constraining, and even constrictive devices. #

The Escape Artist' performance is a superlative of the general capabilities of the Locksmith. So keep in mind that freeing themselves from constraining and even constrictive *places* is often a part of the Escape Artist performance. The Performance Artist is transcendent in general and the initial appearance of the Escape Artist is an example of this. With every new act, the audience did not know what to expect. Considering the inherent risk of coordinating with dangerous devices, unaccommodating places, and dangerously impending restrictions there was always the dual expectation that the Artist could amaze you by getting injured while attempting the difficult process or even perish in the act. #

Another transcendent incarnation of the Escape Artist emerged during the Anti-War protests of North America during its latter unrest circa the mid 1960s. An anti-war Activist and Leader defied bans, curfews and other harassment against leaders of protests by escaping from the constraining place that would be the speaking stage of the Rally or Demonstration. With the complicit obtrusion of his fellow opposition leaders he would speak before the peacefully assembled groups and leave the venue/area without being detected. At some interval, an incessantly "Wanted Man". #

The potential of the Performance Artist to revolutionize the efficiency of sharing ideas that have a Social Purpose should not be underscored. #

We have lately tapped this inertia in the form of viral charitable campaigns. That is, campaigns that are promoted through media-on-demand by informally popular or popularly informal presentations of act. Informal popularity and popular informality are hallmarks of viral media. The supposed virality is actually a euphemism for the hyper-modal tendency of word-of-mouth related to a campaign, performance, candid occurence, slang or (yes) meme. Such performance is often captured without the explicit forewarning of all participant performers. Those individuals walk a fine line because their consent to be the audience of the performance may be negotiable (they often believe they are merely that), but their pending consent to be participant performers is liability. They have recourse to action of removing the media from circulation if they are not satisfied with their presence within the result. #

When the performance is both uninjuring and interesting, most participant audience members enjoy being observably instrumental to the word-of-mouth of a popular act. Charitable campaigns often apply themselves to this phenotypical humanity by issuing an engaging 'Challenge'. The challenge is often as simple as 'make yourself observably instrumental to this popular act'. #

There is a distinction of performance artist that translates particularly well to charitable campaigns that utilize viral marketing. It is The 'Endurance Artist'. On the one hand, the wildly popular ALS Ice Bucket Challenge of just a year or two prior to my writing almost comically invites endurance artistry. The foremost has been encased in ice for hours at a time. The bucket, however, comes and goes within seconds. #

The need to harness popular informality and/or informal popularity, when intending that 'word of mouth' or experiential/participatory marketing take the momentum of your campaign unto itself, can explain the present lack of traction for two campaigns. One campaign more urgent than the other. #

The more prominent campaign can be seen as a diversion from the dire nature of the second campaign we will also mention as a 'blind item'. Hopefully time will permit successful artist to participate and further these causes. The prominent campaign invited its audience to make an attempt to live exclusively within the expense margins of nutritional public assistance rations as endowed to low income individuals and families in various countries including in north America. #

The celebrities who attempted the approximately 20 USD per week diet, free to choose and cook as they pleased, failed miserably at their attempts and were derided in popular social media by web-savvy commenters who surely have never succeeded at such a thing themselves. Popular media was none too kind as well, and much of the commentary seemed to linger on the question of 'why' the "stunt" was worth performing in the eyes of these wealthy and well-fed individuals. The answer should seem obvious, but none was forthcoming. It is not a popular concept in American media that lifting the lower middle class and poorest segment of the population out of poverty is a dire concern. Unfortunately. #

The widespread 'hatred of the vulnerable' in American culture is inevitably endangering the world's ability to assert its own values so long as the U.S. Media machine continues to place all values above the right to nutritious food and clean drinking water. Not to speak of basic medical care. #

A former developer with many investments in emerging markets and a Social Justice blog re Development has discovered the pervasiveness of this problem. As it was recently announced by The World Food Organization and The Food Bank, programs run by the United Nations, that Food

Bank rations are being depleted faster than they are being donated to and allocated to. The result is a very actual requisite for a change in mode of their food distribution specifically in U.N. run Refugee camps. #

The developer Revolutionary of note has taken issue with the 750 Calorie allotment now being rationed to the displaced, traumatized, and previously malnourished United Nations refugees. These are, after all, people who are supposed to be putting their lives back together, essentially, being allotted a starvation ration. He challenges the audience to live for even one week on 750 calories per day. He does so himself and documents/blogs the process. #

In all technicality, that is where the Social Awareness possibilities and emergency support possibilities of the Performance Artist very actually pass into Endurance Artist territory. This is not a "Hunger Strike" and some would philosophize that we should rush to be more receptive to it than we yet do to a hunger strike. It is still yet Art. It is 'Performance' Art. But Endurance Art of this sort carries a more serious risk to the artist and it would be prudent that we employ it to draw attention to serious issues as this developer has done. #

Endurance Artistry doesn't always carry a dire risk. A consistently popular and subcultural European musician is today promoting a performance wherein the artist will produce an album of audio recordings, fully engineered, in an endurance-artist-like enclosure visible to a large observing audience. #

The Endurance Artist as a distinction of performance artist has been of particular attraction to artist who are performers as their mode/medium requites. Another subculturally popular band (a 3-piece) of doctoral music theorists little more than a decade ago performed an act on the eve of and at the turn of the new millenium that lasted to within hours of the length of three 24 hour periods. They rarely stopped to consume/relieve themselves and only occasionally stopped for a modest few hours rest. #

The Endurance Artist came to prominence transcendentally. Not unlike the Escape Artist, one prime manifestation of the Endurance Artist utilized restriction and constriction, and even restraints and the constrains of time etc. The Endurance Acts he performed incorporated a difficulty or peril normally associated as a risk of prolonged exposure to the act in question. Not just physical risk, like the aforementioned encasement in ice, but mental risks such as amazing lengths at perilous heights or difficult lengths under the constant scrutiny of an endless transient audience. #

Performance art like outsider art exist outside of accepted and/or popular artistic supposition and closer to reality. Outsider art is a distinction of two or three dimensional small scale visual art that eschews artistic convention, aesthetic and often medium or material. We won't spend much time on this, but I bring it up because there is an oppositional worthy of note between its evolution and the evolution of Performance Art. To quickly clarify your understanding of outsider art so we can observe this oppositional, let me point this out: Most babies are outsider artist. #

Whereas outsider art's fringe notoriety manifested and evolved from isolation and even confinement; Performance Art's fringe notoriety manifested and evolved from the necessitation of utilizing for an audience people wherever they were found en mass, such as in transit or gathered for another purpose. We will talk more about this in the next chapter. #

Is there a malleable boundary between performance and performance art in linear (i.e. real) time? Is there a malleable boundary between art and performance art? In real time. For the latter, it would merely have to be preconceived and well demonstrated that the art was not meant for audience enjoyment until a certain aspect of performance was incorporated. This could be as simple as preconceiving art into the preparation for a performance or incorporating an audience *en medias res* of a process considered artful in its entirety. #

Final Paragraph:

Consider the exclusion of certain guilded and traditional performers from the overall categorization of artist. Much like the prefixation of street unto artist, performance unto artist should denote a significant and observable elaboration of art in form. It does that precisely in a way that doesn't rely on an elevated conception or consideration. It relies on ingenuity and the desire to challenge one's preconceived definition of art. Considering the reliance on an overwhelming acknowledgment of the art therein, it is the veritable equivalent of the propensity to Disrupt in business models and commercial endeavors. As artist, consider informal popularity and popular informality.

There is no feline-celebrity industrial complex to speak of. In English, there *is* an "urban dictionary" but its user-sourced content and notorious unreliability lend themselves to the informality. The symmetry is not arbitrary. Connecting with people on those levels is good for the process of incorporating art into media and commerce. When an artist finds that certain work acclimates well to word-of-mouth it is important to take the perspective that 'some of the work is being done for you' and to consider how that art might "give back". Social Purpose holds informal popularity in Street Art circles. There is a taboo against too much propaganda or instruction from artist. Therefore, tapping into the natural contagion of popular informality and informal popularity can be used to satisfy the artistic desire to influence action. "Showing" should be de-elevated in our considerations. Teaching must be made an everyday notion prevalent in one-on-one interaction. Demonstration is important of course, but showing people how something simple, brief, somehow challenging, even perhaps enjoyable can be translated into Positive Action and Movement should be a keystone of our study of the potentials of Performance Art.

Chapter 8

Busking

[Busking]

A poet or a musician who spends an entire verse elaborating on an instance is not doing a disservice to the reader or listener. Occurrences and sensations have evitable origins, they have enduring effects, and they have a tangible and complex effect on your person at the moment of occurrence. Providing for elongated study of and/or empathy with such things is hardly a waste of breath or sound. #

It is interesting to note that despite the stark and distinct difference between Spoken Word and Instrumental Music as art forms, we can point out aspects of conveyance that utilize the same term in those two disparate art forms. For example, Tone and Mood. Comparing the utility of analytical terms between those two artforms, and as well between they and *other* art forms, is of particular benefit to a study of Busking. We will do just such. #

Isolating the time to indulge in or partake of poetry, lyricism, or instrumental composition is of a value established beyond the general avail of the listener. It incorporates the valence of leisure to a wider, global population. That population shares a certain maintenent responsibility to their present status/ability to engage in leisure, and to the desire/willingness to surpass that status/expand such ability. Therein, such leisure would be less detrimental to their existence, taken into account as a whole, than it potentially is in that present tense. Such is their Guiding Fraternity with those who can spare less or no time for such indulgence. The Arts require providence. Evitable humanity is merely inhumanity. #

There is only tertiary mention of Fraternity being masculine in the online dictionaries now. Appreciable since guiding fraternity is our best semantic manifestation of the aforementioned. It's interesting that evitable is so much more useful a word than inevitable which is used more often. Barely anything is inevitable. Faculties of the subject in mind, perhaps being born is inevitable. Perhaps dying is as well inevitable. Everything else should well be evitable. Taxes are evitable. #

The world's foremost online encyclopedia outlines the origins of the word Busking by noting it is a derivative of the old Spanish word 'buscar' which means "to seek". It further elaborates that buskers were "seeking" fame and fortune. This is an idealistic view of buskers who, since the dawn of Street Performance, were most of the time seeking the cost of dinner and perchance boarding. #

Street Performance is one of our most essentially human traditions and it has evolved seemingly untouched by the reforms of law. Major metropolitical areas, be they open markets of developing economies or common areas of financial centers, have generally lax regulations on street performance and most do not require license to perform. #

As a Street Artist who is Performing, the Busker takes on a very unique challenge. Performing at an event like a carnival or an establishment like a dining hall have similar challenges, but none other than Busking has the responsibility of rending an audience where, technically, there is none. People encounter buskers as commuters, shoppers, pedestrians etc. So they are in the process of transiting, prospecting, rendezvousing etc. They are not out for their entertainment. The busker's challenge is best described simply: where there is no captive audience, one must captivate. #

In the United States as per its Constitution, busking can not be prohibited in public spaces where other kinds of free speech are not prohibited. That amounts to nearly all public spaces, and exceptions are made almost exclusively for safety. The impeding of traffic flow, both pedestrian and vehicular, is an exemplary safety issue. #

Free Speech and Artistic Free Speech are considered a 'big deal' in North America and many places else as per their respective constitutions. Whereas in terms of Demonstration and political dissent this can be considered a superlative merit of the nations in question and a step forward; In terms of Busking and artistic expression, it is considered a saving grace and a sharp move by the drafting commissions essentially keeping presumed progress from walking over human tradition. The Street Performer is indeed marginalized by the uniqueness of its challenge. #

Modes and mediums of busking vary widely. One could argue that most performance art can be considered busking if the opportunity is presented for the audience to contribute to the performer/s for the performance. Though sharing origins, this is a misconception as performance art has evolved into a complex discipline that is independent of venue. Busking remains contingent on the "primordial" manifestation of the "street" venue and the ambitious rending of an audience where there previously was only a multitude. #

Busking traditionally evolves closely with the integration of politics into the "public" sphere. Not so much the bickering in the senate, but the grassroots movement of which we are all so fond. Although North America may seem like an advanced example of the legislative parallels, it is generally considered there to be legal tokenism compensating for cultural erosion. There *is* an effect on the Art. Around the world the desire to promote and protect shared culture guides legal conformity. Not vice versa. This is evidenced in the enduring global popularity of Spoken Word as a form of busking. #

Whereas Homer, of The Iliad and The Odyssey renown, was surely as enamored as anyone else by the growing sophistication of man-made musical instruments, the revolutions of Instrumental Music in these early eras of record keeping and providence for the arts did not render the Oratorical Poet a sideshow. #

The physical identity of Homer has long been an issue of debate. Argued to be male, female, famous, obscure, learned, uneducated and other such identifiers. It is very recently, within the year of my writing, that the theory has been broached that Homer was not a Person but rather a Way. The argument is that the known oratorical performance, from which we today happen to be graced with hard copy, was in essence a guilded notion. More accurately than 'guilded' would convey, Homer was a "community" notion. Homer was a Tradition. Disproving this may be difficult. #

The advent of enduring instrumental compositions via notation and example did not render oratorical performance obsolete. Along with the obvious coalescence of the two, Busking has traditionally and continually engaged those two art forms more than any other. There are obvious reasons for this, and there are less obvious reasons worth examining. #

Portability is an obvious concern of the Busker. The venue in question doesn't provide loading access for equipment as it is generally a public space. One's potential audience is about, and requesting accommodation as you obstruct the space without pleasing or interesting them will affect your reception. Buskers aim to arrive and make their stage evident/be prepared to perform as quickly and efficiently as possible. First mode of note—Vocal performance of a spoken variety—lends itself well to this. #

Vocal performance of a melodic variety—second mode of note—is a bit more difficult to integrate into these scenarios. It is easier to be interesting (speaking) than it is to be pleasing (singing) especially where bursting into song is more or less the forte of vagrants and disturbed people who inevitably attend the conglomeration of individuals that is the public space. Setting one apart from those who randomly seek attention is important, and where a melodic vocalist might find some success with a PA, some Speakers, Monitors and a Mic, their portability and efficiency is prohibitive. #

Acoustic instruments of all varieties were designed to present their performance to a nominal mass without the need for additional amplification. Such an addition could be and has been of use to a busking vocalist. Its use to—third mode of note—the busking instrumentalist is prime however. The portability of acoustic instruments is generally well considered in their design. Furthermore, the instrument itself is generally visually fascinating and the tendency to observe its workings, as well as the acoustic direction of its sound, help the busker to establish his/her performance space. #

Setting oneself apart from those randomly seeking attention is a facet of 'establishing a performance space'. Being ignored, ostracized or avoided will obviously have a negative impact on a busker's bottom line. The busking orator sets themselves apart primarily by, as mentioned before, being interesting. The creative usage of attire, notes or scripts, props, body language and even amplification tools such as cones or megaphones are all intended to give the casual observer pause and force them to reckon with what they are seeing as original or unusual. #

The dynamics of getting the attention of a preoccupied mass is yet another reason we will focus on Oration and Instrumentation for a length. There are two important ways to acquire the attention of which we speak. Subtly (instrumentation) or aggressively (oration). #

When we discuss Oration or Oratorical Poetry it is important to point out that we are still speaking exclusively of Art. Not Propaganda. It's easy to imagine the Orator stumping enthusiastically for a political cause. It's easy for those without a direct familiarity with the art of Spoken Word to wonder what sets it apart from a raving attention-seeker if not a political cause. They may in fact wonder, what would make them even pause to take notice. #

The tenacity and cohesiveness of one's material is one reason. A Homer would gather a standing crowd by his/her sheer ability to continue on and expertly for hours. That much we know. Creative mechanics of speech is another. Rhyme works quite well for getting attention, if it's patently terrible at keeping it without additional facets of depth. #

Instrumentation when performed skillfully is almost always subtle. One of the beauties of music as an art is the way it occupies its own arena in human cognition. Approaching an orator in a crowd from a distance has a more dramatic process of recognition than approaching previously inaudible music. This informs our understanding of the melodic vocalist and its difficulty functioning usefully in areas of mass gathering, transiting, and commerce. Far too many people have voices and know how to perform the variation called 'singing' for it to fare particularly well either subtly or aggressively. Such is the same reason that subtle oration is ineffective at getting attention. #

Aggressive instrumentation, and such can be achieved, upon initial approach closely resembles things intended to disperse, drive away, or be avoided by pedestrians and crowds: Large machines, dangerous work being performed, sirens, uniquely dangerous calamities. Historically, truly acoustically aggressive instruments have been utilized primarily during street performance of a specific nature. Street parades have often incorporated instruments such as large cymbals played against one another, bass drums so large they need to be strapped to the musician, gongs etc. Like the large groups of musicians that often accompany them, they have the tendency to drive people away. Parades may have been their way of chasing their dispersing audience. Don't quote me on that. #

Tone and mood are elements of artistic composition that translate extremely well between various art forms. In comparing our first and third relevant modes of busking, tone and mood can be observed to be integral elements for connecting with an audience whose emotions can vary as dynamically as the weather itself. Oration, like instrumentation, can establish a tone and/or mood of a presentation very effectively. #

In the study of Oratorical Poetry as Street Art we must avoid dwelling on Victorian and Shakespearean poetry and its immediate predecessors that emerged a good deal after the time of Homer. There are exceptions, but as it is that therein lies the advent of theater as we know it today, the venue was very much intended to move the art form beyond the streets. This is in a way unfortunate because even in Shakespeare's time the performers of his work, especially initially, were peasants who often literally lived on the street. #

The oratorical tradition dates all the way back to the dawn of man in Africa. There, the oral passing-down or teaching of traditional stories remains an important part of many cultures. The tradition itself has been taught and passed-on to prevalence all over the world. We can trace the pathes of Spoken Word and Hip Hop to the ancestral traditions of oration. The tone and mood of hip hop and many styles of spoken word resemble an exponential manifestation of the aggressive call to attention typically employed by grassroots political orators. It has coalesced with art in these forms not by accident. #

Hip Hop is an art form that was born of the streets and its observation on and incisive commentary/admonition/directive toward Social Problems is part and parcel to its purpose as an art form. Hip Hop and spoken word allow us to discuss the viability of politics in busking without sacrificing the supersedence of artistry in our present study. The urban areas of 1980s North America were rife with economic inequality and the ensuing social ills not limited to drug use and rampant crime. No matter how vice-glorifying and apolitical the mainstream American hip hop music industry becomes, there is a larger hip hop industry taking shape all over the globe that has seized on the utility of hip hop for exposing Social Problems and rallying people to seek solutions. #

Hip hop has proven itself universal beyond the boundaries of any spoken language and it has done so as a Street Art contingent on Social Purpose and Social Justice, not as a sensational arena-based spectacle. #

The importance of tone and mood are not lost on Oratorical poets somewhere between a Homer and a modern Spoken Word / Hip Hop artist. One of the most successful (and continually political, if not contiguously or even consistently political) hip hop acts, to whom I've alluded to twice as blind-items, was recently compared by an actor/academic to a certain Walt Whitman in an extensive comparison on the foremost app/website for Literary Notation (in fact for

Notation of any sort as it expands its realm of service). Our compatriot's reasons were sound, but myself and another popular Journo had already assigned Whitman to a different Hip Hop artist while discussing our list of stylistically comparable artist between antique English poets and contemporary hip hop artist. #

At first glance, Whitman resembles any other English poet of antiquity. It is only through careful examination of existing portraiture that one notices the aberrance of his grooming and attire and connects it to his style of poetry. Perhaps his biographies bear easily dismissed indications and humble origins, but unlike his contemporaries Whitman very closely resembles a Street Poet. To put it in reductive terms, he is one of those Orators who might be mistaken for a bum but for his talent. This accurately makes him a torch-bearer for his generation of Street Poet and it is evident in his theatrical style that aggressively establishes tone and mood with impactful opening sounds and words. #

We consider tone and mood for their ability to create an artistic impression that is immediate and contingent to both empathy and a degree of comprehension. Even where empathy is elicited by non-human artistic presentations, people have a tendency to resist that empathy if they can not profess to a deeper facet of comprehension of the artist' intention. As it is that Busking generally requires the participation of a human artist, here note that tone and mood are universal in every form of art even in taking a random example from the simplest 'suprematist school' painting or sculpture. #

Where recognizability (as we mentioned in Chapter 3: 'Ritual Maintain') can circumvent an initial phase of mediatic alienation from the artist and art by an experiencing audience, tone and mood can accomplish the same and can do so for a far more varied demographic. We refrain from forcing a relationship between tone and mood when studying or critiquing a work of art because the boundaries between them are as fluid as empathic emotive between human beings. There is no beginning point for sadness when it is elicited by a work of art. It didn't begin upon observing the tragedy, nor inside of the observer, nor from the similar tragedies previously imparted to the observer, nor from the utter sadness of the tragic figure the observer's imparter encountered. Tone and mood are specific, but fluid observations. #

When tracing the pathes of Spoken Word and Hip Hop to the ancestral traditions of oration, the mutual nature of empathy is evident in the way an artist builds tone and builds mood. Call and Response can be traced all the way back to our ancestral African roots and all the way forward to Hip Hop and Slam Poetry. Wherein the reaction of audiences is important to the success of an artistic presentation, and wherein aggressive vocalization is important to an artistic message, it is prudent to engage an audience and our natural heightened enthusiasm when in a crowd with Call and Response. Sometimes, enthusiasm may lead audience members to attempt to lead a call and response with the artist. It's a much better idea for the artist to take the initiative. So even the ushers can enjoy the show. #

Hip Hop is a good place to introduce our 4th mode of note: Silence. In Busking, silence serves many different disciplines well. A special kind of awe is elicited by Breakdancing done in silence. It is only secondarily done this way in terms of busking, but it is potent and powerful not exclusively in the way that it defies our sense of normalcy. The incorporation of music tempers this sense of shock. The same applies to juggling and other physical feats. #

The Street Art of 'Pantomime' relies on silence. It evolves from an old Franco-european discipline that, once again, was an artistic manifestation of political dissent. The Mime was immune to overreaching laws forbidding the libel or criticism of leaders in power. Laws like this were generally passed at times when artistic expression in the community forum was widespread as entertainment. To avoid squelching popular recreation while protecting their interests against potential brush-fires of dissent, criticism of sitting leaders was time and again banned by act of law. The mime was skilled in the art of mocking the elite, even seemingly specifically. #

The mime overcame the hurdle of silence by commanding attention with unusual attire. Stark black and whites became the uniform representation of the mime along with ghostly white facepaint and expressive black markings around their eyes. Their physical movements also commanded attention, much the way breakdancing and contortionism do, with the sheer propensity to go from normal to exceedingly unusual and back again with seemingly little effort. #

To work well in the Busking arena, any form of dancing generally verges on transcendence of traditional dancing and dances. In dancing to profit from tipping in public, it remains true that it is more viable to be interesting than it is to be merely pleasing. A Performance Artist we should note for its inextricable relationship to busking is the Human Statue. Human Statues are skilled in making their movements so minute and exceedingly deliberate that sans inspection they would be mistaken for a person standing absolutely still, or an actual statue. It is with elongated observation, usually a few minutes, one notices difference in composition between time points. Human Statues are usually identifiable by a contained platform perhaps bearing plaque, and often by being covered in metallic, grey or luminous body-paint and/or attire. #

Most all of our mentioned 4th mode of note disciplines qualify as transcendent dancing. This is not to minimize stilt-walkers, hula hoopers, and sword swallowers. They are traditional characters that are often times more Performer than Artist. Busking demands ingenuity to keep audiences presenting tips, which they will not do easily once a wonder becomes commonplace or homogeneous in its manifestations and their routines. We will entirely ignore costumed characters that pose with guests for photos and for tips. Though they are reported to be exceptionally skilled at the art of swindling. #

Breakdancing is an archetypical Street Art and our consummate dance discipline. Classical dance (predominated by ballet), ballroom dance, modern dance, hip hop dance and African dance are all dependent on a musical movement or tradition. Hip hop dance shares that with breakdance though it has evolved into a large-venue discipline often experimenting with synchronicity. The notion that there should be a discipline referred to as "Street Dance" is questionable. Club Dance might advent to discipline as per Electronic Dance Music. World Dance or better World Beat Dance would showcase the evolutionary successor of Afro Beat music. Hip Hop dance is today what Modern dance was for many decades. Breakdancing aside, if you are dancing to hip hop music, pay the respect. If you are dancing in the Street to Pop music...I have a lot of questions. #

Breakdancing is as well the prominent introduction of portable stereo systems into the field of Busking. Whereas out of doors, most viably acoustic instruments are larger than a portable stereo system, the system can produce the sounds of all of those instruments, volume notwithstanding. Consideration needs to be given for interesting your audience (many of whom have stereos of their own) and for power sources. Amplification of a system in a public arena generally requires a stronger power source than is required to play the stereo in one's home or in a smaller enclosed space. Exceptions exist and apply to many instruments, devices, and even techniques, such as Busking in acoustically viable places like Subway platforms. That is, of course, until the train arrives. #

Final paragraph:

Consider that through the procession of this chapter it is evident that the most useful reasoning for the busking of an artist' wares was the interaction between the artist and a paying audience. In the event that an artist is performing only live music and not encouraging the bootlegging of and profiteering from the live performance, the product the artist is purveying is in fact the live performance. It is in the nature of busking performances that the interaction of "tipping" 'in good will' supersedes the notion of charging a structured price for the enjoyment of the live music (or live spoken word). Dancing and other forms of artistic entertainment are even less likely to have a set price structure in the event that the performance goes down in an open venue such as municipal commons. The transactory interaction of the artist with the audience can be determined in advance—a cover charge, for example—or in an impromptu nature, requests for donations is a common technique. Establishing the willingness of the, daresay, "captive" audience to pay the performer/artist for his performance tends to appreciate the performance in the eyes of those tasked with minimizing the use of public spaces for solicitation. However, that interaction can not preclude or lessen the importance of providing performance of artistic work in good will and free of charge, as is tradition. The public forum itself should maintain with recreation including performance and informal trading. For the audience, this is good for business on every end of their excursion or commute. The Busking concur.

Chapter 9

The Marks of Passage

[Passage]

Integrity and loyalty. This is a basis of democracy and most forms of governance. The two are why such systems work. When it doesn't work, it is because people are giving and breaking their word. They are receiving in return for their word, yet compromised by that reward. In the Socratic ideal, officials got no campaign contributions for their promises. The devotion of the people to rise and fight as well for no particular wage was the eventual reward. That is the basis of the republic. The reward is the provident peace in which they would exist. #

Integration has a distinct denotation relevant to many multi-cultural communities and nations. Politically it refers to the process and time-frame wherein individuals from different cultural backgrounds began sharing the space and time occupied by their social systems. #

Integration in the poli-scientific sense was important to less vocationally distinctive social processes like education and leisure services. Academics is a more specific synonym for education and it is used more often the further along a subject is in academic process. Consider that the resistance to integration was strongest outside of academics, and to a relevant degree within and without of higher academics and its circles. To some degree, because the standard in Higher Academics is to foster when needed, but not to teach 'agitation'. This has generally been reinforced institutionally in hindsight to the culminating events of the civil rights and anti-war era of 1960s North America. What is the reason that we, in basic education, were more open to cultural differences than our elders? What might we have done, at that age, to acclimate the period of integration and avoid its frequent incarnation typified by resistance? #

If some feel discontent at the thought of their vulnerable state of childhood. It is prudent to assume this is symptomatic of their desire to have a voice in the prevalent values of and, more importantly, the governance of their social structure. Abiding by governance established in distinct departure from their preference may lead some to thinking they were, as children, morally superior to that which they have committed themselves to as adults. This is primarily if they are one of the Voting Public. They believe the perceived ills they have accepted and compromised to would vex their child self. #

People living in a society require governance of their social structure. Disagreement between individuals is most peacefully juried, adjudicated, and legislated by constituents and civil servants selected by a voting body. To go about fancying flesh and bones and projectile weapons as solutions to disagreements is deviation from civil society. #

Integrity, can refer to the well integration of decision making within an individual. That is the very voice they exercise when casting their vote or demonstrating their objection. It is the permeation of internal resolve that maintains one's word. It is not the internal caprice of aggravated action. Personal physical strength or force does not arbitrate or legislate faithfully. We as well know that if we ever rely on brute and weapon to exert personal will, that society in which we peacefully exist would object and seek to legislate or adjudicate in opposition to our actions or even our favor. #

The notion of a superior moral state in children is only to be taken literally if the word 'state' is taken in a legal sense. The minor's superior moral state is accompanied by an inferior political state. It is worth noting that young children do innately have a more stringent moral resolve which can be weakened by the observation of negative stimulus as they grow older. "Bullies" for example are known to have more negative stimulus in their lives away from school than their peers. #

Religion and Superstition are two things that stem the decay of moral resolve in an individual's development. The former institutionally structured to do so, and the latter through coincidental encounter and respondent conditioning. #

It is prudent to take a look at the general connotation of defiance and resistance. As well compare and contrast internal moral rigor vs external moral rigor. Defiance of one's compelling body can hardly be accomplished without a forethought path of arbitration. #

In an attempt at bypassing established governance, lacking integrity will ultimately result in reversion to a childlike state. In evading democratic process and/or the responsibility of civility, one often dotes on one's moral self. Partly because we believe chance and spontaneous fortune are more frequently loyal to moral integrity. Affecting lasting meaningful change relies on the fortune of actions. Evading established governance relies on the fortune of actions as well. While deliberate prevalence in social systems is often achieved by a reliance on integrity and loyalty, social Change is reliant on a very present and enduring sense of moral integrity. #

By 'deliberate prevalence' in 'social systems' we refer to the prevalence of an individual, not necessarily of an individual's will. By nature, social systems require mutual validation for any individual to be accurately an effective component of the system of reference. An individual's will as it functions within a social system intends to influence others and the will of others to coincide with it for the, individually presumed, greater benefit of the greater social system. We do this by example, admonition/ostracization, litigation, and legislation. #

Individual heterogeneity is not so much 'originality' and our Social Systems are not mitigating originality nor creativity that is beneficial to the Social System. There is great and obvious benefit for the species that maintains shared values and inclinations. The integrity and loyalty that are a condition of, and contingent on, an individual's social prevalence are a microcosmic representation of our human will for our greater social systems. Within our communities and political systems, the Stewards of Change must prove themselves to have in bounty the permeation of internal resolve that maintains one's word. They must prove themselves to superlatively lack the internal caprice of aggravated action. #

In many ways, this text is concerned with change on a very basic level. Change within an individual is microcosmic to change within an individual's social settings. Art has long explored the effects of an individual's environment on that individual, and as well the effects an individual has on their environment. Street Art is distinctly and instinctively revolutionary within artistic disciplines in the way it presents its discussion of change. #

Our value for our Art and Architecture is culturally enduring in nature. This has naturally carried over to the installation of Industrial Art in corporate settings. When constructing our structural surroundings, there is the intention that structures should outlast any single generation of the people who rely on them. When selecting artwork to adorn our structural surroundings, there is the intention that appreciation for the artwork selected should live on beyond any single generation of the people who experience them. Even as historical media. #

Street Art arrests the abstraction of the discussion considering an individual's effect on his environment and vice versa. Street Art is often an individual's deliberate impression on his/her very environment. Street Art thus contingently makes bold and overt statements on the environment's effect on individuals. It's worth noting that Live Installation, that is Installation Art that is observed by an audience as it is rendered into place, is not limited to temporary works created to incorporate or utilize the characteristics of a certain location. It can apply to mural art, industrial art, etc so long as the Installation is witnessed for its Artistic Value. #

As it is that we shun caprice when displaying works of art 'for posterity', change in the representative artwork of a social setting is both macrocosmic and microcosmic. They are macrocosmic of the will of an individual or individuals adventing or consensing. They are microcosmic of the less observable changes, as per the consensus and advent of individuals, that manifest in our social systems and are guiding constructs in our social existence and communities. Taken individually, they are Symbolic. #

An individual's deliberate impression on their mind and body are of concern in this chapter as well. Do not concern disproportionately with basic forms of conditioning. We concerned ourselves previously with responsive conditioning in Chapter 2 'Masochism'. The process of incorporating incentive into the responsive nature of self-stimulative masochism would lead to the complexities of operative conditioning. They are simple in the matter of thinking, but could be complex given the layover between pleasure vs admiration of pain. Social Learning Theory takes conditioning a step further. #

Learning is a form of conditioning that is known to elicit reactions that involve numerous cognitive behavioral responses. Namely attention, retention, reproduction, motivation yet such could be conjuncted in various ways. Entrancement that is reproductive of simple choreography wouldn't necessarily qualify as learning; but synthesis, which doesn't require isolated attention, would. #

Adornment of our structural and natural surroundings with works of art, while intended to be ceremonial and steadfast, is most frequently performed in places where meaningful change occurs or is fostered. Likewise deliberate impressions on an individual's own mind or body that are artistic in nature are symbolic of and instructive of change. #

The artistic marks one leaves on their own mind are no less a relevant mark than the artistic markings we make on our bodies. The process of leaving that deliberate and valent mark is more cognizant than that of the masochistic marks we leave on our mind. The semantic ambiguity of The Marks of Passage is due to the dual microcosmic/macrocosmic nature of art in our personal lives & personal space and our public lives & public space. #

The most frequently occurring way to leave a deliberate artistic impression on the mind is to experience a work of art. Creating a work of art can do the same but it is widely preferred the artist provide a comparable experience for the audience and it should as well be comparable if the artist takes part in audience. #

For mental impressions, the valence of those impressions is tantamount to utility and thus relevance. Deliberately subconscious impressions are self-sublimation and not of concern in The Marks of Passage. As with body art, we are concerned with impressions on the mind that are valent not just to the individual, but to be shared and/or experienced by others. #

Access to our mind's store of previous experiences is limited. That is to say, memory fades. Thus merely experiencing a work of art is not enough to definitively warrant the distinction of 'deliberate artistic impression on the mind'. Even dance theater can be entirely forgettable. The valence of such impressions is contingent on cognitive processes. Mostly. #

Simply experiencing a film does not guarantee valence of artistic impression. However, 'method film criticism' if such a thing were to become "a thing", would. Like method acting the intensive counterparting of the experience to comparable experiences in the individual's life creates a valent artistic impression. #

Our method film criticism would likely be considered performance art since popular media Critics have bastardized artistic criticism to the point where criticism isn't considered an art. Good criticism is an art. Artful criticism at no point requires negativity in any shape, form or fashion. #

Memorization, mantras, and the recollective techniques of various art-therapies all create valent artistic impressions on the mind. But the mind has, and people have, ways of initiating deliberate valent artistic impressions. Autonomous Sensory Meridian Response is a particularly interesting one. The illusive agency of its cognitive process, like that of numerous simple emotional responses, also makes it party to the "mostly" I concluded with three paragraphs prior to this. Tonal memory response is similar to ASMR in its cognitive behavioral process. Music therapy relies on tonal memory response and does not exclude simple emotional responses. #

One can utilize one's person to leave an artistic impression on others. In the same vein, one can utilize models. The valence of a deliberate artistic impression on the mind is important if one intends the art to have a lasting impression. Memory fades. Whereas masochism is often utilized as a form of conditioning, artistic impressions on the mind that don't rely exclusively on pain are a form of learning when instructive of change. This can be instructive of a change that has taken place or of times, areas, and arenas of one's life where change takes place. #

The same is true for deliberate artistic impressions on the body such as hair & makeup artistry, tattooing & piercing, traditional marking & bejeweling, and garment design. All of these art forms inherently concern with change. We reserved the discussion of utile accessories for Chapter 6. #

Times, areas, and arenas of one's life where change takes place are often paralleled between peers in our social systems. Schools are attended at certain ages. Licenses for driving, marriage etc are issued at similar stages. Parks become indispensable to families of similar phases. Art, entertainment, leisure spaces, local commerce, these things initially gave *to* the lives of people who, in maturing, decide to give-back in the same way. Beautification can be as important to the mental well being of the young and senior citizens as education and enduring inclusion. #

Communities that permit and even commision public art and murals—in particular, are known to be less ageist and ableist than their counterparts. Paying heed to human Character Development at *all* stages of life is natural to Art, Public Art and its Champions. #

In education and learning, the model is more than just a clothes-horse or human canvas. Facets of a model's character are examined during the cognitive behavioral process of learning. Just the same in art, facets of a model or performer's character can be examined during the cognitive behavioral process of experiencing art. Experiencing a work of art does not preclude learning. Attention, retention, reproduction and motivation can be necessary to fully experience a work of art the way an artist intends. This can be as simple as an artist' intent that the audience remember the name of a performer or model. #

Final paragraph:

Consider the ways in which an individual's artistic tendencies and/or physical appearance inform the observer about the individual's character. Deliberate artistic impressions on the mind don't always manifest observable "tendencies". Thus consider the desire in an individual to be able to communicate what it perceives about a person's character. To convey as accurately as possible, we tend to incorporate artfulness into our discussion of character. Imagine, for the sake of example, you find yourself surrounded by many people who exhibit behaviors that are inane, hysterical, and heedlessly fanatical. To create an impression for someone who is unfamiliar with it or oblivious to it, we can use any or all of those words. But to create a visual artistic impression of that character is far more difficult. Part of the beauty of social interaction is mystery and surprise. People don't necessarily advertise their depth of character. Salutational movements, graphic or conversational clothing, distinct expressions, comfort objects, imitative personal style; these are a few digressions from tattoos & piercings, traditional marking & bejeweling, and hair & makeup artistry. They, and other learned or acquired visual identifiers can be utilized to introduce facets of identity when generating character. Rarely will the elongated isolation we discussed in 'Masochism' be the ensuing saga of your generated character. So consider how your character will be perceived with and interact with her or his community and artistic community. No need to stop after this book is over, continue to consider Character Development every time you engage Character Creation. Especially when you will play as a character for many hours in improvisational documentary media or a video game. There should be a synergy taken into account because there *will* be a synergy. Character Development is not something to attribute to young children alone. That is the mentality of a society that encourages one exclusively to Conform after a certain age. It's a sort of ageist fascism designed to tinker with the personalities of children, deny the propensity for growth and learning into middle age and beyond, and sell books to the captive readership of pregnant women and new mothers. How does a friendly middle aged woman or man develop into an angry miser? As you engage the character synergy in The Street Artist Method, you are microcosmic to the generating of your community's character.

Chapter 10

The Conservant

[The Conservant]

A study of the nature of Conservancy observes Passivicity in its many incarnations in Social Systematics. Consider that causing a thin layer of metal-oxide that prevents further rusting is generally a singular and one-sided goal thus we speak of Passivation, but only occasionally Passivicity. Engineers and electrochemists who deal with currents, complex valence etc, can hypothetically find value in observing both the activation and deactivation of Passivation. #

Likewise, electronic engineers may need refer to changes in Conductivity when engineering that which is practical and utile vs observing that which is aberrant or coincidental (i.e. a change in conductivity). Perhaps such will become the standard now as graphene has been found to go from insulator to superconductor when a simple superlattice (two layers of it) is rotated at a minute & precise angle. #

Tellingly, Green Engineers who deal with Passive Design can and have felt the need to focus on Passivicity. #

Any system of doing things utilizes energy in the process. To apply the tenets of conservancy we must be aware that there is resistance within the executive cycle of any process. Maximizing efficiency while tending to the Greater Sustainability and the Greater Humanity can be seen as the Conservant's goal in applying passivicity to a process. #

Applying passivicity to a process may in itself maximize efficiency. This is often the case with small scale mechanical processes. As well with small scale systems composed of mechanical processes. It is a known intention of computational process. Ecosystems are great examples of passivicity applied to process, specifically where plant life and weather systems are dominating factors of an executive cycle. #

Automation has certain bounds where the Conservant is concerned. In automating a process, we take something that was previously done through one process and allow it to be done through another process that requires fewer or no human decisions or actions. If the process was previously a facet of an occupation, it can make the worker's job easier. It can require the worker to alter his process and/or learn new skills. It can obsolete a worker's involvement in a specific process. #

Careful consideration is required before implementing more advanced forms of automation. Maximizing the efficiency of a worker requires a humane approach. Repetitive facets of an occupation are most detrimental to the mind of an individual the more limited the decision-making and the less qualitative the feedback. That variety of repetitive task creates within a person a stress rooted in occupational validity. Tasks with an inherent risk to a worker create within a person a stress rooted in fear-of-harm and anxiety. Tasks with inherent difficulty in satisfactory accomplishment, create within the worker a stress rooted in negative qualitative feedback. #

Automation of the three previously described kinds of tasks, should maximize efficiency without burdening the worker with an inordinate degree of additional stress. Altering one's process or learning new skills can create additional stress. The stress can be inordinate if a manager or trainer is not made available. The avail of a manager or trainer to assist in the incorporation of automation should be considered a low-cost high-yield expense. #

The Greater Sustainability of an enterprise, as in other areas of coexistence, involves maintaining one's workforce and expanding it with the natural expansion of the enterprise.

Altering a job process, incorporating new techniques, mastering new skills; all can have a positive impact on worker morale and a minimal addition to worker stress if engaged with humanity and sustainability in mind. Obsolescence of a worker's occupation takes neither the Greater Humanity nor the Greater Sustainability to heart, wherein no or too few alternative duties or occupations are provided during automation. #

The Academic is an integral part of a complex system that applies passivicity to process. Within our social systems, we consider academics to be low-cost high-yield expenses. There is passivicity inherent in the process of allowing for an individual to teach many individuals at the same time. #

There are a great many factors consistently existing in the workplace that create stress. Such is in the modality of a process being accomplished by an individual. These factors can create inordinate stress if allowed to become too frequent or too contingent on the need for a difficult to detect requirement of qualification. Giving qualification is a consistent duty for most workers who take part in a process. It may be as simple as taking note. It may require a contingent action. #

Neglecting to note a requirement of qualification can cost a worker his job. Neglecting an action contingent to a qualification may cost a worker his job even sooner. Any repetitive action has the capacity to disrupt a worker's sense of occupational validity. This includes a hyper-frequency of requirement for qualification and/or contingent action. When the sense of occupational validity is compromised a worker may lose his job due to factors that emerge outside of work, outside of the specific process, or even while they are executing the specific process. #

It can be assumed and evidence has shown that carefully reducing a worker's stress increases productivity. Carefully applying passivicity to process thus inherently increases productivity. It increases efficiency by reducing the worker's reliance on coping methods that can be time consuming and sometimes cost the enterprise an entire day of work from that particular worker. While productivity is a concern for most enterprises, efficiency is often engaged only opportunistically and often entirely pretentiously. Efficiency is a concern of both the Greater Humanity and the Greater Sustainability. #

Conservation of one's own physical energy is just one way conservancy manifests. Applying passivicity to process can, at its most basic, reduce the amount of physical energy exerted by a worker and inherently make his/her job easier. #

The accelerated permutation of self that is individual occupation does not, in our social systems, base its validity on the degree of exertion (mental or physical) that is required. The tiers of qualitative feedback a specific profession receives are intended to aide in the competitive advancement of the entire field. Our present economic structures are notoriously inempathetic when it comes to weighing the value of employees against advancements in efficiency. #

The conservant, as much as artist and professionals who are concerned with social justice and social purpose, is concerned with disparity on a very basic level. On a basic mathematical level, disparity is a tell-tale indication of insustainability. #

It has become desirable as of late, for a CEO to have the vision of his/hers being a Vertically Integrated enterprise. Vertical Integration as a business model emerged as the compassionate, consumer-conscious method of mitigating supply and demand and benefiting from it. Vertical integration holds in low regard the social-engineering of Artificial Demand. The model has proven itself to be competitively profitable without artificial demand. #

A "Vertically Integrated Enterprise" in the vogue of recent visions seeks to be provident to natural demand in as far-reaching, even dynamic, an incursion into a market and related markets. Once they become major contributors in a market, the companies of concern—rather than fall prey to the temptation of socially-engineering artificial demand—would seek their greater revenue by expanding their offerings in the market and into related markets. This is disruptive thinking—in the vogue that disrupting capitalism is positive—considering that markets can be "related" by notions as simple as sensory medium. #

The reality of Vertical Integration and dynamic development in general, makes it plainly evident that the denotation can not be reduced to 'In-House' versus 'outsource'. It must be studied as an emerging and self-defining reality. Millionaire simpletons will attempt to appropriate the label to justify their monopolistic gambits. Venture Capitalist take note, development can not be winner-take-all forever. Not without changing the handle from development to "compelling-body consumption" or "fat-cat-own-tail-eating" or something. More on Dynamic Development in *Creative Direction*. #

Thus conservant thinking is concerned with disparity in enterprise on a very basic level. One of the core merits of modern enterprise is expounded to be the mutual benefit to all parties involved. Doubtlessly, big business' penchant for paying its executive officials far more than its general workforce is an exemplary manifestation of disparity in enterprise. The conservant sets that notion aside to seize on the comparative disparity of pathetic job-creation numbers and utterly inhumane mass-layoffs. #

The competitive profitability of vertical integration and the untapped, and likely excedent, profitability of the "vertically integrated enterprise" is a clear indication that mass-layoffs are not just utterly inhumane, but entirely unnecessary and logistically detrimental to a company's bottom line. A company's revenue statistics and a company's market value are not a subjective responsibility. Economics is incessant and ceaseless give and take and an executive is tasked with representing the interests of regulating governments; vendors, contractors & franchisees; often advertisers; often shareholders; *as well* as clients and customers. But that is not where responsibility begins in enterprise. #

An enterprise can not have rational concern for the Greater Humanity if the interests of its Workforce are not its foremost concern and responsibility. Layoffs notwithstanding, job-creation as well would not be as sluggish as it has been of late (and specifically in the world's biggest economy) wherein conservant regard for sustainability and consequently humanity is applied more frequently to business models. #

Vertical Integration is just one distinction within a business model that exemplifies the application of conservant principles. In manufacturing, the process of providing evenly and voluminously for customer demand is generally considered less expensive. The processes needn't be altered as frequently. The tools needn't be altered, augmented, or replaced as frequently. The risk lies in a lack of understanding of or empathy with your engagors and a subsequent overabundance or overprevalence of unpopular merchandise, services or applications. #

It is worth noting the difficulty in utilizing the phrase "vertically integrated company" to speak of the Revolutionary intent of being a part of a Vertically Integrated Enterprise. Vertical Integration of an entire enterprise integrates the entity into potential markets. Vertical Integration in its simplest form integrates goods produced by a company into the market. These companies generally produce greater quantities of uniformly similar items, and consequently must pay more acute attention to the needs and desires of its customers. The general internal goal of transitioning to the new intent is to have greater oversight of quality and availability. A globally sourced enterprise can chose to vertically integrate a single product. Interrelationally and thus Ethically, Ecologically, and Economically a company's incentive in transitioning to the new intent is vast and adventing. #

The Revolutionary intent of Vertically Integrated Enterprise diversifies not only goods provided but potentially services and even market of reference. In this way, the Vertically Integrated Enterprise has a natural propensity toward steady and lasting job creation. The overall company growth of well executed entry into a new market is intended to be much greater than if the same number of new employees were added to merely grow the company without market diversification. The job security of such vanguard employees can be projected to be greater than that of the latter examples we just described. Unless the undiversified-market new hires were already for a market experiencing rapid growth. But bear in mind emerging markets are by definition in a state of rapid growth. New markets by distinction are, much the same, engaged expressly regarding the potential for rapid growth. #

The individual formally known to possess the highest figure of private monetary wealth [Update: surpassed by final edit] has repeatedly admonished his fellow investors as having their priorities misplaced. When it comes to problems facing humanity, the issue of sustainability as an integral consideration to one's business model isn't merely a moral one. When established markets and emerging markets face health, climate, and humanitarian difficulties the viability of a market, or all markets, can be diminished or even annulled. #

As he presently pledges 2 Billion USD of his around 79 Billion personal fortune to Research and Development agencies, he has referred to the private sector as "generally inept". Developing clean energy sources, for example, doesn't hold the jackpot allure that keeps venture capitalists investing disproportionately in eventually failing companies. (One wonders why his health related investments would tend in opposition to Democratic Socialist Healthcare.) #

In order to be hailed as an academic example of a disruptive enterprise a company must succeed, at the least, in changing the way their competitors view and engage a market. This kind of change is inherently conservant in nature. The low-energy high-yield process of tapping into a previously underrecognized engagor sentiment is the conservant core of market disruption. #

When entering new and emerging markets, it is prudent for businesspeople to recognize that consumer sentiment (let's use engagor sentiment) is inextricably linked to cultural sensitivity. The prospired definition of Conservant ethic must encapsulate all three considerations aforementioned. The most effective allocators of our resources, our energies, and our cultural sensitivities must all be studied. #

An example of disruptive allocation of resource in business, would be the executive who recently granted every individual employed by his company a base pay of 70,000 USD. The rationale is that employees work better when their morale is high and their life away from work is secure. The high-productivity, low-turnover, minimized human-resourcing budget etc... It may yet prove to be conservant allocation. #

Disruptive allocation of energy is as simple as relying on and investing in Clean Energy Sources. Furthermore Clean Energy is Conservant Energy. The American company that mass produces exclusively All-Electric cars is the paragon of enterprise that is both Disruptive and Conservant. #

An example of Conservant allocation of our cultural sensitivities that is as well disruptive in its utter originality, is the doing of the founder of the "public-face changing application" mentioned in Chapter 1. It was not when they purchased the photo-sharing application mentioned previously to be democratising art, and moves like that face-washing are reasons to be cautious. This is a company that hopes to change the entire internet by making it accessible to people in emerging markets and poor communities all over the world. What was once a method for transitioning the internet into a social organism, will soon spawn a structured and massive introduction to the internet. Thus the introduction of 2G Tuesdays to his employees is intended to create an inextricable cultural sensitivity for the people of emerging markets and their yet modest modem speeds. Monopolistic doubts notwithstanding. #

Recently the practice of Search Engine Optimization was referred to in a major media publication as "a new Art". SEO or maximizing the visibility of your propriety when a search is made through a search engine, requires modes of thinking that are unconventional to traditional business practices. It requires a humanist approach to the way that people use language. Considering the ceaseless evolution of locution, parlance, style etc, it requires an artistic approach. It is no accident that my present search for a synonym to colloquialism brought up, in addition to the three in the previous sentence, many familiar and many complex words. Among them 'street talk'. The way that people use language is a cultural sensitivity. #

Considering the high demand for and endless prevalence of advertisement in media and in our physical space, it is prudent to compare it to SEO. Targeted advertisement that invades an individual's privacy in order to advert to them things they are presumed to like based on the tracking of their interests, has been implemented for a number of years yet it has not been shown to observably reduce the high-waste modest-yield ratio of advertising in general. Fortunately, this is nearly intangible waste in the digital era (wasted money notwithstanding) but advertising as a sector of industry has been notoriously slow to evolve. SEO looks to be an evolutionary competitor of traditional and even targeted advertisement. #

Artist, who spend their entire practice exploring the nuances of appealing to the human senses and the human mind can doubtlessly tell advertisers to "Wake Up". Traditional Advertising is like playing a bird call of one species and hoping to attract many species. Search Engine Optimization is playing the right bird call to the right species every time. #

Consider advert demand. That strange and rare occasion where engagors demand advertising typified by the yearly phenomenon of North American Superbowl Commercials. Those 30 second increments between football game activity is some of the most expensive advertising "real estate" on earth. It is also the few hours on television per year that engagors are generally confident they will be genuinely entertained and engaged by commercials. That is sad. #

Cultural sensitivity is a prudent consideration most specifically when any group or aspect of commerce moves into a previously unfamiliar or emerging market. But it should also be applied to most any Movement or mass-media pop-culturism. #

The failure of advertising companies to elevate their standards of creativity when moving from magazine & billboard to radio & television are evident today. Their move was accompanied by a culturally insensitive commandeering of the way people took in their entertainment. There is a similar cultural insensitivity at play on the internet and in web connected mobile devices where ads that "pop up" obstruct content, delay content, and distract the eye are rampant. When engagors are empowered with a recourse to action, the tables will inevitably be turned, revenue will be lost, and advertisers must go back to the drawing-board. This is evident with DVR, TiVo etc 'ad skipping' capabilities, and with the million-dollar pit-fights at hand over 'ad blocking' applications. #

There is the misconception that Pop-culture has a blank slate to promote itself on, that there is no other culture to which it owes sensitivity. Pop-culture is notoriously insensitive. It is, in fact, a commercial culture intended primarily to promote consumerism and weaken any foundations that do not promote consumerism and fortify capitalism. The outrage of both indigenous and immigrant cultures to various pop-culture overtures has surfaced time and time again. The danger is perhaps greatest now as society has come to accept the boundary pushing of pop-culture specifically when it has gotten to the point of bringing its desired desensitivity practices to the mainstream and the "primetime" as it has been called. #

The glorification of violence; of indiscriminate homicidal proclivity; of voided compassion for any considered strangers; of hysterical ridicule of individual's traits, appearance, characteristics, handicaps, ideas and behaviors; of misogynist exploitation; of capitalist exploitation; of idolization of the wealthy; of idolization of the despotic; all of these are being allowed to permeate our media with little objection. #

The ideals of the conservant doctrine have parallels and roots in various socio-scientific arenas. The Conservant itself, however, is a wholistic application intended to be a useful modality in a permeant and perpetual way for the individuals who engage it. #

The Civil Rights movement of the 1960s in North America saw an effective and momentous manifestation of Conservant ethic in the advent of Passive Resistance. When speaking of Passive Resistance, the necessity of analyzing Passivicity and not Passivity resounds. #

The Reverend/Doctor who led much of that movement was in no way alone in time nor place in his sentient utilization of it. Many, many Nonviolent Peaceful Demonstrators both activist and activist leaders kept stride. Furthermore, Civil Disobedience, Sit-Ins, Hunger Strikes and the like have been the tools of Revolutionaries all over the world. #

Applying passivicity to political disruption, however, has its limits. This is true more than ever in the aggressive political climate where discrediting and deterring activists have become the major weapons of those who maintain a financial interest in protecting the status quo. #

There has been little recourse to the pepper-spraying of Nonviolent Peaceful Demonstrators who were in fact sitting silently in a circle on a college campus in the U.S. There has been little public outcry to the violent dragging of a teenage girl, who did nothing more than sit quietly in her desk, by a campus officer. There has, in fact, been a response by the head of a national association known to endlessly instigate violence and protect the violent behavior of certain population segments that it was justifiable for the girl to be 'treated like an animal' because she 'acted like an animal'. Perhaps a three-toed sloth. #

As Fascism gains traction, one of the things one notices is the disdain fascist have for the free will and autonomy of those who threaten their interests. The forced altercations in the last paragraph, and laws such as the highly disputed "Stand your ground" law serve a similar deep-seated desire in those who perform and evoke them: The desire for jurisdiction over the physical movements of another person's body. Considering the aforementioned law is carefully taken into consideration even before the need arises to "stand one's ground" it can be considered an exit strategy for those who seek to control the movements of others. It can embolden them to antagonize others or to attempt to dictate the behavior of others. It dramatically emboldens them against any resistance to their orders, which are not sanctioned nor requited by governing bodies in most cases. It essentially encourages vigilante-ism. #

In politics and government where the mask of docility has given way to aggression and incensing rhetoric, Proactivity is the most appropriate modality. But the case remains that if one falls prey to oppositional political forces by their use of physical instigation, unjust detainment, or unlawful surveillance,

Conservant action should be immediately employed in the interest of preserving the individual. #

Activism performed from a place of imprisonment is inherently Conservant. Prisons are intended to break the will and spirit, as well as dramatically limit one's resources, so this is an area of concern where Conservancy strays most closely to a spiritual practice. Maximizing the influence of the detained self through targeted open media is advisable. Minimizing idleness and maximizing time and influence through Narrative Argument and Artist Expression is advisable. #

The semantic manifestations of words with the root word Conserve are many. Conservancy is more frequently used as part of the proper name of Organizations tasked with protecting wildlife or resources. Conservism however doesn't serve our purposes for the same reason that Passivity does not evoke the full potential of Passivicity. #

The Passivity of a passive house alone would invoke little of its utility. But in alternately using energy, its overall Passivicity is able to conserve far more energy than traditional structures while achieving similar levels of comfort under various weather conditions. Its mere passivity might be useful to a sound engineer looking to map the trajectory of a sound's waves through a complex space. #

Conservationism is a human-centric way to think about Sustainability. The voluntary protection of nature for future human use is becoming a dated notion. Environmentalism is a nature-centric way to consider Sustainability and it is rooted in

Humanity. Humanity is not a self-placent or profit-seeking notion. Protecting nature from the greedy, reckless, and profit-hungry requires we utilize our social systems of government to enforce Regulation. #

Conservator can well be the legal manifestation of the need for nature conservancy in human social life. The promotion of the longevity and well engagement of the otherwise incapacitated and their estates is much like the duty of organizations with the proper name Conservancy. #

Conservatories take the same mode of thinking and apply it to our Artistic Evolution and Artistic Heritage. To throw out all the old ideas and dazzle the world with new ideas is explicitly contrary to the Conservatory's wisdom. Where a Nature Conservatory is concerned, it is as well illogical to raze a landscape and import new plant life and animals. It overlooks the full breadth of ecosystem including weather cycles and microbiology. #

Conservatism may be the least dynamic semantic manifestation beyond conservism if we assume "conservism" amounts to "hoarding". Conservatism in politics primarily preaches fiscal responsibility but doesn't necessarily practice what it preaches. It maintains that those who have always benefited the most from government policy can offset whatever growth and gain are required and desired with the robust and joyous spending and hiring they will do when they are catered to. It is quite literally the political doctrine of "Resistance to Change". It is the status quo that is there "Conserved". #

Structural Conservatories (small annexed greenhouses) again recall the Passive House. The principles and complexities that keep the passive house energy efficient are the same principles that were noted in the conservatory annex that often was used for a library, study, or studio. When heating structures or cooling structures was very difficult, the option of a glass walled room fared easily and well. Often on those days when the base structure required much energy and effort. #

The primary intention of Conservancy in relation to an individual's energy and influence, is not to "save" or to "preserve", it is to Generate. It is no coincidence that we can apply our usages as valid parallels in this concern. It is natural. The laws of nature dictate that "preservation" of species and ecosystem must be accomplished through "generation". Likewise, the academic conservatory is not primarily to "preserve" the relics and methods of previous lifetimes. It is to teach Artist and Musicians valued knowledge that will assist them and enable them in becoming the greatest new talents among their peers. The conservancy/conservatory "as place" is also intended to Generate. #

Final Paragraph:

Art is by nature Conservant. Exploring the nuance of appealing to the human senses and the human mind inevitably requites the audience's overwhelming acknowledgment of art therein, but rarely expends its resources in an aggressive or exhausting way. When dissecting that denotation above, the Greater Humanity and The Greater Sustainability can momentarily abandon their permeant persuasions to grant us the clarity of a rudimentary relationship that a child can grasp and that echoes as a maxim of great depth. "I create Art of Greater Humanity. Therefore, you are not hurt." and "I create Art of Greater Sustainability. Therefore, I am not tired." Once we have mastered our core Conservancy, as Street Artist, we can then consider ourselves the foundation on which Proactivity can be built. As important as it may be to be Proactive our primary sociological duty is to be Artist and to instill our Artistic values in others young and old. This does not preclude activism. Teaching however is a low-energy, low-risk, low-cost x high-yield expenditure. The notion of Proactivity itself favors organizational labor over protestation. Rendering oneself confined or banned does not satisfy all the requirements of Proactivity. In this interconnected age one should be able to raise awareness or crowdsource support as effectively as was formerly the domain of lobbyist and PR. Within just the past two years we have seen in North America an acute and vigilant focus in popular media on injustice as resulting outrage has proportionately manifested on popular social media. Activism is no longer perfectly typified by invoking "Lawful Excuse" or the "Necessity Defense" when climbing a smokestack in Kent to paint a Prime Minister's name on it. Power in numbers is ever more powerful in the age of interconnectedness. With the spreading of Humane and Sustainable values through Conservant Proaction, these numbers will yet become unassailable. Thoroughly developed realistic representations of ourselves are teaching tools that Artist should apply where mindless brainwashing characters once stood. Incorporate those numbers. To be Just. To be Green. A new way remains. If you Be it, they will Change.

www.ingramcontent.com/pod-product-compliance
Lightning Source LLC
Chambersburg PA
CBHW071043240526
45471CB00014B/391